N I N E
plus

NINE
plus

TAKING THE LIMITS OFF YOUR GIFTS

JOAN HUNTER

Copyright © 2021 by Joan Hunter

Published by Hunter Books

PO Box 411

Pinehurst, TX 77362 USA

www.joanhunter.org

978-0-9988739-4-7 (print)

978-0-9988739-5-4 (ebook)

Scripture marked AMP is from the Amplified Bible. Copyright © 2015 by The Lockman Foundation, La Habra, CA 90631. All rights reserved. Scripture marked ESV is from The Holy Bible, English Standard Version. ESV® Text Edition: 2016. Copyright © 2001 by Crossway Bibles, a publishing ministry of Good News Publishers. Scripture marked KJV is from the King James Version, which is in the public domain. Scripture marked MSG is from *THE MESSAGE*, copyright © 1993, 2002, 2018 by Eugene H. Peterson. Used by permission of NavPress. All rights reserved. Represented by Tyndale House Publishers, Inc. Scripture marked NASB is from the New American Standard Bible®, Copyright © 1960, 1971, 1977, 1995, 2020 by The Lockman Foundation. All rights reserved. Scripture marked NIV is from THE HOLY BIBLE, NEW INTERNATIONAL VERSION®, NIV® Copyright ©1973, 1978, 1984, 2011 by Biblica, Inc.™ Used by permission. All rights reserved worldwide. Scripture marked NKJV is from the New King James Version®. Copyright © 1982 by Thomas Nelson. Used by permission. All rights reserved. Scripture marked NLT is from *Holy Bible*, New Living Translation, copyright © 1996, 2004, 2015 by Tyndale House Foundation. Used by permission of Tyndale House Publishers, Inc., Carol Stream, Illinois 60188. All rights reserved. Scripture marked TLB is from The Living Bible copyright © 1971 by Tyndale House Foundation. Used by permission of Tyndale House Publishers Inc., Carol Stream, Illinois 60188. All rights reserved. Scripture marked TPT is from The Passion Translation˙. Copyright © 2017, 2018, 2020 by Passion & Fire Ministries, Inc. Used by permission. All rights reserved. ThePassionTranslation.com. All marks of emphasis in Scripture quotations (bold, italics, all caps) are the author's.

Thanks to Naida Johnson Trott, Nathanael White, and David Sluka for their valuable assistance with this book.

Cover design by Yvonne Parks at www.pearcreative.ca

Interior design by Katherine Lloyd at www.thedeskonline.com

Printed in the United States of America

21 22 23 24 25 5 4 3 2 1

contents

PREPARE TO BE ARMED AND DANGEROUS

*I*f you are a Christian, God is your heavenly Father who blesses you daily with life and breath. Everything in life is supplied by our Creator. Everything we need to complete our God-planned assignment and reach our destiny is available.

He supplied communication to guide our path ages ago. For instance, God will take a message straight out of the Bible and make it applicable for where you are now and for the people you meet with each day. I want what I am going to say in this book to walk through your natural man into your spirit man. It will fill you up in the natural so much that you will not be able to contain it. You will feel compelled to share this message with others.

Nothing will keep you from doing what He wants you to do. God is tired of His people giving Him excuses. He's tired of hearing the words, "I can't," because His Word says, "I can do all things through Him who strengthens me" (Philippians 4:13 NASB).

The Passion Translation puts it this way:

> I know what it means to lack, and I know what it means to experience overwhelming abundance. For I'm trained in the secret of overcoming all things, whether in fullness or in hunger. *And I find that the strength of Christ's explosive power infuses me to conquer every difficulty.* (Philippians 4:13, emphasis added)

What would you do if you could have that explosive power working within you? Would you act differently? Would you do things a new way? Since we are instructed to act like Christ, do you think your human abilities would change, perhaps even soar? Would you choose to act more like Him?

IF JOAN CAN, YOU CAN!

Many people knew my parents, Charles and Frances Hunter, who are with the Lord now. So often they repeated the statement, "If Charles and Frances can do it, you can do it, too!" My words are slightly different. "If Joan can do it, anybody can!"

My mom and dad were geniuses. Basically, there was nothing that they couldn't do. I am honestly glad I missed the genius gene. There is a lot more pressure that goes with the "genius" title. I was told I was dumb, stupid, ignorant, and retarded. In my younger years, no one believed I would be able to read or write, yet I have over twenty-five books published as of this writing and there are more coming. That's pretty awesome! God wrote them. I was simply His obedient conduit to get His messages into print to travel around the world to His children. This is God's explosive power to conquer every difficulty.

I want to encourage you that, "If Joan can do it, anybody can do it!" I believe that I missed the genius gene as a part of God's plan so I can present His plan in simple terms so everybody can understand it. The only complaint about my teachings has been, "I didn't know it could be this simple!"

So many people try to make salvation difficult. They believe the Bible message is so hard that they won't even read a few Scriptures. They may classify supernatural healing as impossible, imagination, or unbelievable.

Escape this kind of thinking. Your next step is to hear from the Holy Spirit and allow Him to guide you through the next chapter in your God-ordained Christian walk.

> For all who obey his commands find their lives joined in union with him, and he lives and flourishes in them. We know and have proof that he constantly lives and flourishes in us, by the Spirit that he has given us. (1 John 3:24 TPT)

> And he has given us his Spirit within us so that we can have the assurance that he lives in us and that we live in him. (1 John 4:13 TPT)

God has such detailed plans for your life. He has people in place to help you understand His ways and His Word. Don't block His communication like Moses tried to do. If Moses had not listened to God and obeyed, the Israelites could still be slaves in Egypt.

Exodus 4:10–16 (NKJV) tells us this story, saying:

Then Moses said to the Lord, "O my Lord, I am not eloquent, neither before nor since You have spoken to Your servant; but I am slow of speech and slow of tongue."

So the Lord said to him, "Who has made man's mouth? Or who makes the mute, the deaf, the seeing, or the blind? Have not I, the Lord? Now therefore, go, and I will be with your mouth and teach you what you shall say."

But he said, "O my Lord, please send by the hand of whomever else You may send."

So the anger of the Lord was kindled against Moses, and He said: "Is not Aaron the Levite your brother? I know that he can speak well. And look, he is also coming out to meet you. When he sees you, he will be glad in his heart. Now you shall speak to him and put the words in his mouth. And I will be with your mouth and with his mouth, and I will teach you what you shall do. So he shall be your spokesman to the people. And he himself shall be as a mouth for you, and you shall be to him as God."

GOD WANTS TO WORK THROUGH YOU

Moses begged the Lord to send someone else to speak to Pharoah. God got angry with Moses. Remember, anger comes from unmet expectations. Moses did not meet God's expectations and God got angry. God didn't like Moses' excuse "I don't talk very good!"

If someone asked you to speak at a meeting at your local church, would you say, "I can't speak well"? God tried to send you to a foreign country. What was your excuse? "I don't know how to speak that language?" God says, "I'm sending you to represent Me! I will not make a fool of you and will not allow you to make a fool of Me!" How can you say no to God?

God prepares you for what He assigns you to do for His kingdom. He designed you specifically to accomplish something special in His world. You may not feel qualified, but God calls you qualified anyway because He is with you. You may not think you are prepared, but He has prepared you from your birth. He will never send you anywhere or ask you to do something without His preparation or supplying what you need to be successful.

God usually places someone in front of you who needs exactly what you can offer them, such as salvation, healing, love, or deliverance. You were once that needy, hurting person and He sent someone to help you. Now you are the one with the answers. He will send you to another...and another...and another. You just have to be willing to reach out, speak a word, and touch someone with God's love.

Get rid of the excuses. How can you apply what you read in this book? If someone is hobbling in pain in front of you, believe God brought them to you at just the right moment. You don't have to muster up the anointing or stop to pray. Just reach out and touch that person. A few words or a short prayer is all it takes. Don't take on the responsibility of their healing. It is not your responsibility if they get healed or don't get healed. That responsibility is God's.

Human wisdom will never understand the Spirit, but God needs you! He needs a few good people who are willing to do what the Word of God says. Old, young, men, women, and even children can be and are used by God. For example, His Word says to "lay hands on the sick, and they will recover." He doesn't specify size, shape, sex, or nationality. You simply have to be willing.

> "They will take up serpents; and if they drink anything deadly, it will by no means hurt them; they will lay hands on the sick, and they will recover." (Mark 16:18 NKJV)

The devil is the enemy and needs to be afraid of you. You don't need to be afraid of him. As a Christian, you have been reborn with Jesus, and He is living in and through you. In addition, His Holy Spirit now lives within you. The enemy needs to tremble when you wake up in the morning. God and Jesus are a lot stronger than any devil! You need to get that in your head and believe in your spirit that you are indeed *armed and dangerous*!

Get rid of the spirit of fear. Fear attempts to hinder your faith and block your path. Faith will encourage you to do what God calls you to do. Through this book, you will learn the important tools God gives you to fight your battle. Jesus is victorious over sin, death, and the devil. You can also be victorious. Remember, God always wins.

GOD WILL WORK, EVEN IF YOU'RE AFRAID

There was a young man on the front row in a service (I will call him Mark). He obviously had a broken arm because it was in a cast. I prayed a simple prayer for him and told him when the cast was taken off the next week, there would be only a hairline fracture.

By a word of knowledge, I called for someone who had a broken bone. A 35–45-year-old man raised his hand. He had broken his leg both just above the ankle and below the knee, and he was still in a lot of pain. I asked Mark to pray for him. Mark was ten years old and was terrified to get up in front of all the people. Being in front of me (whom he had seen on television) didn't help. He certainly didn't believe he could pray for someone else and see them healed. The older man could have gotten upset at a ten-year-old who didn't know what he was doing.

I encouraged the young man, but he felt like he was getting pushed to the front. I repeated the verse from Exodus, "God will give you the words to speak!" I said, "Repeat what I'm telling you."

Finally, he came up and laid his hand on the man's damaged leg. He repeated the words I gave him, cursed the spirit of trauma and pain in the name of Jesus, and thanked Jesus for doing the healing. The guy was totally healed!

God will give you the right words at the right time. (Matthew 10:19 NLT)

The Sovereign LORD has given me his words of wisdom, so that I know how to comfort the weary. Morning by morning he wakens me and opens my understanding to his will. (Isaiah 50:4 NLT)

Jesus said to him, "I am the way, the truth, and the life. No one comes to the Father except through Me. (John 14:6 NKJV)

Before going any further, if you have any doubts about your relationship with Jesus, pray this prayer:

"Father God, please forgive me for all my sins, the times I ignored Your voice, and when I went my own way. I need You and Your guidance in my life. I can't do this alone. In fact, it would be silly to try to accomplish things without Your input and help. I accept Jesus into my heart and into my life. Jesus, please live in me and work through me. Touch others through my voice, my hands, and my example. I choose to make you the Lord of my life. In Jesus' name. Amen."

As you study this book, you will discover that the illumination of the Holy Spirit in you will open your mind by faith to receive His gifts. It is in the Word of God and Word of God is truth.

If God said it, it will happen, and all you have to do is to step into the stream of power that God wants you to have. You will move into this supernatural dimension and discover your Garden of Eden.

As you absorb the principles in this book you are going to

walk into the supernatural, a new dimension that your flesh cannot understand. However, your spirit will know exactly what to do.

HOW TO USE THIS BOOK

Now, it is time to get to work. God has provided the tools for you to use under His direction. Remember, He will not ask you to do something without the provision to complete the task.

I believe this unique book on the gifts of the Holy Spirit is a valuable tool. Read, learn, and share it with others. Let His message go viral. Use this book to equip you for ministry to others, to answer questions, and more.

Questions highlighting the important points are located at the end of each chapter. I highly encourage you to take time with these questions so you can truly absorb these truths deep into you where they can and will change you into a powerful weapon in God's hands.

Finally, there is an index of subjects at the end of the book, which will make using this book much easier. Keep this book with you as you minister, and if any question comes up, just invite them on the journey of discovering the answer together.

Now, let's go, in Jesus' name!

chapter 1

THE STORY OF GOD'S HOLY SPIRIT

The Holy Spirit did not suddenly become active on the Day of Pentecost. Quite to the contrary, He was active in the Old Testament, too. Some people don't understand this, because most discussions about the Holy Spirit are primarily based on the Book of Acts. But, if you do a study on God's Holy Spirit, you will find He was busy many years before Jesus was born. Let's examine what He did through the Old Testament.

God's Holy Spirit was present at creation. Genesis 1:2 (NKJV) says, "The earth was without form, and void; and darkness was on the face of the deep. And the Spirit of God was hovering over the face of the waters." This is as early in history as anyone can get—the very beginning. Yet we see that even then, the Holy Spirit was both present and working.

God filled men of the Old Testament with His Spirit for specific tasks. In Exodus 31:1-6 (NKJV), artisans for building the Tabernacle were blessed with God's anointing to help them in their task. This is a perfect example of God's provision for completing what He wants man to accomplish:

> Then the Lord spoke to Moses, saying: "See, I have called by name Bezalel the son of Uri, the son of Hur, of the tribe of Judah. And I have filled him with the Spirit of God, in wisdom, in understanding, in knowledge, and in all manner of workmanship, to design artistic works, to work in gold, in silver, in bronze, in cutting jewels for setting, in carving wood, and to work in all manner of workmanship. And I, indeed I, have appointed with him Aholiab the son of Ahisamach, of the tribe of Dan; and I have put wisdom in the hearts of all the gifted artisans, that they may make all that I have commanded you.

Also, while many today seem to place the Holy Spirit on the sidelines during the period of the Old Testament, Job recognized the Holy Spirit and gave Him credit for his life and breath:

> The Spirit of God has made me, and the breath of the Almighty gives me life. (Job 33:4 NKJV)

GOD'S COVENANT PROMISE

Our Old Testament forerunners and foundation-layers knew the Holy Spirit was for them, and they prophesied how important the Holy Spirit would be for us. They even said He will live within you and all your descendants:

"And this is my covenant promise with them," says Lord Yahweh. "From now on, my Holy Spirit will rest on them and not depart from them, and my prophetic words will fill their mouths and will not depart from them, nor from their children, nor from their descendants, from now on and forever," says Lord Yahweh. (Isaiah 59:21 TPT)

David knew through the Holy Spirit he had God's favor. He wanted to please his Heavenly Father and couldn't imagine being without God's help from the Holy Spirit. Obedience is key in this!

Create in me a pure heart, O God, and renew a steadfast spirit within me. Do not cast me from your presence or take your Holy Spirit from me. Restore to me the joy of your salvation and grant me a willing spirit, to sustain me. (Psalm 51:10–12 NIV)

Keep creating in me a clean heart. Fill me with pure thoughts and holy desires, ready to please you. May you never reject me! May you never take from me your sacred Spirit! Let my passion for life be restored, tasting joy in every breakthrough you bring to me. Hold me close to you with a willing spirit that obeys whatever you say. (Psalm 51:10–12 TPT)

The Holy Spirit was not just present and active here and there through a few people. No, He was so important in the

Old Testament that even the king of Babylon recognized Him working in Daniel (this is Nebuchadnezzar speaking):

> "And then Daniel came in. His Babylonian name is Belteshazzar, named after my god, a man full of the divine Holy Spirit. I told him my dream. 'Belteshazzar,' I said, 'chief of the magicians, I know that you are a man full of the divine Holy Spirit and that there is no mystery that you can't solve. Listen to this dream that I had and interpret it for me."

> 'This is what I, King Nebuchadnezzar, dreamed. It's your turn, Belteshazzar—interpret it for me. None of the wise men of Babylon could make heads or tails of it, but I'm sure you can do it. You're full of the divine Holy Spirit." (Daniel 4:8–9,18 MSG)

What a testimony from someone who had been surrounded by magicians and people who were powerful through demonic witchcraft his entire life! He knew none of his gods and none of his magicians could answer the problem he faced. Only Daniel—empowered by the divine Holy Spirit—could unravel the mystery.

PROPHECY THAT JESUS WILL HAVE THE HOLY SPIRIT

We've seen that the Holy Spirit was present and active in Creation. He anointed various people at times for particular tasks. Old Testament followers of God knew their need of the Holy Spirit, and the Holy Spirit was key to both God's covenant with His people and their ability to serve Him.

All this culminates in an incredible promise: when the Messiah comes, even *He* will need the Holy Spirit:

> Then a Shoot (the Messiah) will spring from the stock of Jesse [David's father], And a Branch from his roots will bear fruit. And the Spirit of the Lord will rest on Him—The Spirit of wisdom and understanding, The Spirit of counsel and strength, The Spirit of knowledge and of the [reverential and obedient] fear of the Lord. (Isaiah 11:1–2 AMP)

> There shall come forth a Rod from the stem of Jesse, and a Branch shall grow out of his roots. The Spirit of the LORD shall rest upon Him, The Spirit of wisdom and understanding, The Spirit of counsel and might, The Spirit of knowledge and of the fear of the LORD. (Isaiah 11:1–2 NKJV)

In the Old Testament, when God spoke to a prophet like Ezekiel, Daniel, Elijah, Moses, or one of the great men of old, He communicated by His Spirit. Sometimes God spoke audibly, sometimes through angels, and sometimes through visions and dreams. Whatever the manner, God would speak to His prophets and give them a message He wanted delivered. These persons were recognized as the spokesmen of God to the children of Israel. These people were called prophets and would often say, "The Lord God told me to tell you this."

That means this word of the Lord about the Messiah came through the Holy Spirit and was about not just the Messiah, but also the Holy Spirit. The Holy Spirit was telling us that part of how we would recognize God's Promised One is He would have the Holy Spirit. How's that for the importance of the Holy Spirit!

GOD'S PERSONAL PROMISE TO ME

The next passage from Isaiah in the Old Testament is one of the foundational Scriptures of Joan Hunter Ministries. If I didn't believe every word with every fiber of my being, I couldn't do what I do. By myself, I can do very little. With God's love, strength, and wisdom, I can travel the world and share His promises to you. I lay hands on you and fully expect you to be gloriously healed in Jesus' name.

I invite you to read, pray, and bury these words into your heart as you step forth to follow and work for your heavenly Father:

> "The Spirit of the Lord God is upon Me, because the Lord has anointed Me to preach good tidings to the poor; He has sent Me to heal the brokenhearted, to proclaim liberty to the captives, and the opening of the prison to those who are bound; to proclaim the acceptable year of the Lord, and the day of vengeance of our God; to comfort all who mourn, to console those who mourn in Zion, to give them beauty for ashes, the oil of joy for mourning, the garment of praise for the spirit of heaviness; that they may be called trees of righteousness, the planting of the Lord, that He may be glorified." (Isaiah 61:1–3 NKJV)

And I do glorify my God with every prayer I pray and every song I sing. I worship Him with my every breath. I expect you to lay ahold of every promise God has spoken, to know that He speaks truth and will bring it to pass.

GOD FULFILLS HIS PROMISE—HIS NEW COVENANT

We have so far barely scratched the surface of the Holy Spirit's work in the Old Testament, yet we saw that it all culminated in God's promise to send His Messiah, anointed and empowered by the Holy Spirit.

As soon as we step into the New Testament, we see God begin to fulfill His promise:

This is how the birth of Jesus Christ took place. His mother, Mary, had promised Joseph to be his wife, but while she was still a virgin, she became pregnant through the power of the Holy Spirit. (Matthew 1:18 TPT)

Mary questioned the angel who visited her. How could she even become pregnant while still being a virgin? But the angel explained:

"The Holy Spirit will come upon you, and the power of the Highest will overshadow you; therefore, also, that Holy One who is to be born will be called the Son of God." (Luke 1:35 NKJV)

I don't know if that made sense to her, yet it remains an incredible statement. It wasn't the only problem, however. She was engaged to be married, but this union had yet to be consummated. Being pregnant at her young age would cause many embarrassing questions within her family and community. Would her betrothed still want to marry her?

When Joseph needed encouragement to maintain their engagement, God sent an angel to reassure him that Mary had remained pure:

> An angel from the Lord appeared to him and said, "Joseph, descendant of David, don't hesitate to take Mary into your home as your wife, because the power of the Holy Spirit has conceived a child in her womb." (Matthew 1:20 TPT)

THE PROMISE AND PROPHECY OF JOHN

At about the same time Mary had her miraculous encounter with the Holy Spirit, Mary's cousin Elizabeth had been barren, but God blessed her with a promise. She was going to have a son, whose name was to be John. Mary and Elizabeth were both pregnant about the same time:

> And you will have joy and gladness, and many will rejoice at his birth. For he will be great in the sight of the Lord, and shall drink neither wine nor strong drink. He will also be filled with the Holy Spirit, even from his mother's womb. And he will turn many of the children of Israel to the Lord their God. (Luke 1:14–16 NKJV)

When John was grown, he lived in the wilderness, declaring to the people:

> "I indeed baptize you with water unto repentance, but He who is coming after me is mightier than I, whose sandals I am not worthy to carry. He will baptize you with the Holy Spirit and fire." (Matthew 3:11 NKJV)

> "I indeed baptized you with water, but He will baptize you with the Holy Spirit." (Mark 1:8 NKJV)

Can you begin to feel the momentum of God's promise building? The Holy Spirit stirred in Creation, empowered the Old Testament saints, promised the Messiah—and now the promise about the Messiah is He will give *everyone* the Holy Spirit!

JESUS' BAPTISM IN WATER AND THE HOLY SPIRIT

First, however, Jesus had His own baptism. When Jesus wanted to follow the designed path for His life, He went to His cousin John for this very purpose. John recognized Jesus and was humbled by His request:

> Then Jesus left Galilee to come to the Jordan to be baptized by John. But when he waded into the water, John resisted him, saying "Why are you doing this? I'm the one who needs to be baptized by you, and yet you come to be baptized by me?"

Jesus replied, "It is only right to do all that God requires." Then John baptized Jesus. And as Jesus rose up out of the water, the heavenly realm opened up over him and he saw the Holy Spirit descend out of the heavens and rest upon him in the form of a dove. Then suddenly the voice of the Father shouted from the sky, saying, "This is my Son—the Beloved! My greatest delight is in him." (Matthew 3:13–17 TPT)

What an incredible truth! If Jesus needed to be baptized and receive the Holy Spirit's help to fulfill His destiny and purpose, don't we also need Him to help us? We are to be like Jesus. I believe the help of the Holy Spirit is vital to successfully spreading the Gospel and living the Christian life.

Jesus lived His life and worked all His miracles by the power of the Holy Spirit. He then prophesied to believers who needed to prepare for the future to come. You can count on His promises and base all your faith on the Word of God and His covenants.

Living water has long been used as the description of His Word which lives within each believer. Believe in Jesus and you, too, will receive the wonderful gift of "living water" which flows from within your soul:

"Believe in me so that rivers of living water will burst out from within you, flowing from your innermost being, just like the Scripture says!" (John 7:38–39 TPT)

This living water is one of the great promises Jesus gave us. Even more, however, is His promise to give us the Holy Spirit,

20

who is nothing less than God Himself filling us with His very own being. Once He lives inside us, He promises that He will never leave us or forsake us:

> Loving me empowers you to obey my commands. And I will ask the Father and he will give you another Savior, the Holy Spirit of Truth, who will be to you a friend just like me—and he will never leave you. The world won't receive him because they can't see him or know him. But you know him intimately because he remains with you and will live inside you. I promise that I will never leave you helpless or abandon you as orphans—I will come back to you! Soon I will leave this world and they will see me no longer, but you will see me, because I will live again, and you will come alive too. So when that day comes, you will know that I am living in the Father and that you are one with me, for I will be living in you. Those who truly love me are those who obey my commands. Whoever passionately loves me will be passionately loved by my Father. And I will passionately love him in return and will reveal myself to him." (John 14: 15–21 TPT)

If you have believed in Jesus, then you have this very same Holy Spirit living inside you. Let those words sink in deeply, because nothing could be more life-changing than this single truth: God lives inside you!

He will teach and guide you. He will comfort and heal you. He will shape and empower you, ultimately making you more and more like Jesus. This is His goal for your life, and it is why you will need the Holy Spirit as you enjoy a life filled with signs, wonders, and miracles.

> But the Advocate, the Holy Spirit, whom the Father will send in my name, will teach you all things and will remind you of everything I have said to you. (John 14:26 NIV)

> Now may the God of hope fill you with all joy and peace in believing, that you may abound in hope by the power of the Holy Spirit. (Romans 15:13 NKJV)

thoughts to ponder

* Which instance of the Holy Spirit working in the Old Testament is the most surprising to you? Why?

* Which promise in Isaiah 61 do you want working in your life? Why?

* How many words can you think of that describe the Holy Spirit, such as Friend, Advocate, Teacher, Helper, Protector, or Guide?

*   What is a covenant?

*   What promise has God made to you that you are relying on Him to keep?

chapter 2

FIRST THINGS: SALVATION AND HOLY SPIRIT BAPTISM

*E*ven though the emphasis of this book is centered specifically on the gifts of the Holy Spirit, I want to remind you of something very important: God's gifts He has planned for you started before your birth. He is the life-giver Who planned and orchestrated your existence. He chose your parents and the place and time of your entrance into this world. Everything you see, hear, feel, or touch is truly a beautiful and wondrous gift from God.

Your friends, talents, abilities, and desires are all precious blessings (gifts) from Him. Pastors, teachers, family members (parents, grandparents, siblings, spouses, children, grandchildren, etc.) are included in the "gift" list. The next time you get irritated with someone or a situation, remember God placed you exactly where He wants you to be. Maybe God is teaching you one of His principles today; or perhaps you are supposed to help someone else learn about God and His love. Absorbing just these two paragraphs can change your life.

God uses people to do His work here on earth. He used them throughout the Old and New Testaments, as you learned in the first two chapters of this book. God hasn't changed. He continues to work through people—through their hands, feet, and especially voices as they share His Word.

God's first instructions to Adam and Eve were to care for His garden (the world) and go forth and multiply. I believe that instruction still holds true today (see Genesis 1:28).

Since God knew man couldn't get things together throughout the Old Testament, He promised that the Savior would come to help. God waited many years for man to straighten up and act right. Of course, men neither agreed nor behaved. God spoke through His prophets for years before Jesus arrived. If you study the Scriptures, you will find several prophets talking about the One Who was to come—Jesus.

Sending His only Son to earth as a baby was such a wonderful way to introduce Jesus. He had to learn to talk, walk, play, and work just like everyone else. I am sure Jesus played and roughhoused just like a typical boy and came home to Mary with a scrape, bruise, or bump. His earthly body experienced the same things we have through our lifetimes. Aches, pains, joys, and victories are not isolated only to us. He suffered. He cried. He loved and laughed. He bled and died.

Even Jesus needed help. He knew His assignment from His Father and was confronted with an almost impossible mission. We sometimes have to learn the hard way to depend on God. The big difference with Jesus was that He knew where His help came from—His heavenly Father and all His angels. We are still learning about our dependence on God, Jesus, His Holy Spirit, and the angels.

THE GREAT COMMISSION

Jesus could only be in one place at a time while He lived on earth. He must have felt a bit frustrated since He was certainly not limited while He was in heaven.

He knew He had to multiply Himself by training His followers so His Word could spread. As the earthly body of Jesus today, we have to do the same. As we witness and allow His gifts to work through us, we are manifesting Jesus to people we touch. We, in essence, have to multiply ourselves also by sharing the salvation message with others as Jesus instructed us to do:

> Then Jesus came close to them and said, "All authority of the universe has been given to me. Now wherever you go, make disciples of all nations, baptizing them in the name of the Father, the Son, and the Holy Spirit. And teach them to faithfully follow all that I have commanded you. And never forget that I am with you every day, even to the completion of this age." (Matthew 28:18–20 TPT)

To fulfill the Great Commission as Jesus commands, we need everything possible to help us. His assignment for us to reach the world (all nations) can be quite daunting and overwhelming. That's why we must not be naïve. No human can fulfill that command by themselves.

Jesus couldn't physically reach everyone in His world by Himself. We can't either. Jesus assembled His team and sent them out to reach the masses. We have to follow His example. He didn't leave His followers without promising and sending His Holy Spirit to assist them. That same promise reaches through the centuries to you and me. He didn't leave us powerless or helpless.

God's Spirit magnifies our understanding of His grace and love. This powerful connection between God and man empowers us to hear and obey what our Father wants us to do during our time on earth. God loves all His creation, especially all His children. Using His wisdom and working through us, He can reach His kids. We must remain open and obedient to His voice:

> For we did not receive the spirit of this world system but the Spirit of God, so that we might come to understand and experience all that grace has lavished upon us. (1 Corinthians 2:12 TPT)

JESUS AND HIS HOLY SPIRIT

Each of us has a part to play within every situation. How boring life would be if we all talked alike, walked alike, looked alike, and acted alike! No, God made an exciting world with so many different variables for us to enjoy and learn.

Within the body of Christ, there are also many parts. Every person has their own individual assignment. God then provides what each person needs to fulfill their assignment. The special gifts from the Holy Spirit facilitate that assignment. Don't ever believe your talents and abilities are developed by your own desires and hard work. God gave you everything. What you do with those abilities, however, is up to you. I'll talk more about that in the chapter, Developing Your Gifts.

This kind of personal development is rarely free. How much is this power, wisdom, and more going to cost you?

Well, a gift is free; otherwise, it is a purchase. Remember when we were talking about all the gifts God has blessed you with from birth? Some call them "blessings," but no matter which word you use, they are free gifts from your Creator.

"We are witnesses of these things, and so is the Holy Spirit, whom God freely gives to all who believe in him." (Acts 5:32 TPT)

Every gift God freely gives us is good and perfect, streaming down from the Father of lights, who shines from the heavens with no hidden shadow or darkness and is never subject to change. (James 1:17 TPT)

God also bearing witness both with signs and wonders, with various miracles, and gifts of the Holy Spirit, according to His own will? (Hebrews 2:4 NKJV)

So answer me this: Did the Holy Spirit come to you as a reward for keeping Jewish laws? No, you received him as a gift because you believed in the Messiah. (Galatians 3:2 TPT)

For the wages of sin is death, but the gift of God is eternal life in Christ Jesus our Lord. (Romans 6:23 NKJV)

You have not done anything great enough to earn any of God's gifts. The gift of the Holy Spirit is not earned either. God provides His Spirit so you and I can spread His Word and draw more of His children into His Kingdom. God knew we couldn't fulfill the Great Commission on our own.

HOW TO RECEIVE

Some people received the Holy Spirit baptism the very moment they got saved. At that point, they may or may not have ever heard about the Holy Spirit or what would happen. Only God knows when He chooses to bestow this gift upon anyone. Most often a person has said the salvation prayer, has perhaps already been baptized, and then heard there was yet another step. Regardless of how it often happens, God can choose to give you His Holy Spirit whenever and wherever He pleases.

Many have questions, however, about how, when, what, why, or where, and that's one thing this book can be used for. Your questions can be answered, or you can use this information to share with someone who has the same questions you had before you received the Holy Spirit baptism.

I'm about to answer those questions, but first, know that wherever you are right now, God can meet you there. You can receive the Holy Spirit wherever you may be. Years ago, my father received the baptism of the Holy Spirit with evidence of speaking in tongues as he was driving home from work.

Another lady I know of received it while lounging in a bathtub with candles flickering on the counter.

Of course, the very first step is salvation. Repent, believe, get baptized in water, and then ask for the baptism of the Holy Spirit.

> Peter replied, "Repent and return to God, and each one of you must be baptized in the name of Jesus, the Anointed One, to have your sins removed. Then you may take hold of the gift of the Holy Spirit. For God's promise of the Holy Spirit is for you and your families, for those yet to be born and for everyone whom the Lord our God calls to himself." (Acts 2:38–39 TPT)

Life with the Holy Spirit starts here—with salvation. Now let's work through the other questions, starting with the step we must take once we are saved.

Ask: The first step is to desire all that God has planned for you. If you truly desire to serve Him and live a committed life for Him, you will need His help to accomplish those plans. Ask Him sincerely to bless you with His Spirit. Open your heart and wait. Some receive immediately, some don't. But God always fulfills His promise.

> If you then, being evil, know how to give good gifts to your children, how much more will your Father who is in heaven give good things to those who ask Him! (Matthew 7:11 NKJV)

"If imperfect parents know how to lovingly take care of their children and give them what they need, how much more will the perfect heavenly Father give the Holy Spirit's fullness when his children ask him." (Luke 11:13 TPT)

When: God has His special timing for each of us. It will happen probably when you least expect it to happen. Remain in anticipation. It will be a life-changing experience which you will never forget. It can happen at any time, either day or night. A friend woke up in the middle of the night speaking in tongues. Another was praying out loud and suddenly couldn't understand the words they were saying; they were speaking in tongues.

The baptism in the Holy Spirit is not limited to church or a meeting. My dad ministered the baptism of the Holy Spirit to thousands at one time during his and my mom's years in ministry. God blesses in His timing. Don't hold God to just one way to do what He wants to do.

Who: Any Spirit-filled believer can minister to you and pray for the baptism of the Holy Spirit; however, it often occurs at a service where a pastor lays hands on you. Just realize that God is in control, and He will give it to you at His perfect time. Meditate on His Word. You can also receive by praying for it all on your own. Ultimately, God is the One Who baptizes you with His Spirit whether you are alone or in a group.

And they were all filled with the Holy Ghost, and began to speak with other tongues, as the Spirit gave them utterance. (Acts 2:4 KJV)

How: Often, it can be imparted by the laying on of hands. It can, however, happen anytime. You can be waiting in the back of the church and receive at the same time as someone else who is being ministered to at the altar. Just desire and ask. I often hear a special word being given and I simply say, "Father, I receive that word for myself also." Sincere desire is the most important.

God can transfer His gifts through you to somebody else or maybe through somebody else to you. You can be the receiver of a gift from God through other believers. You may have had prophecies spoken over you before you understood what they were. That communication could be the reason you are now being drawn to learn and experience more.

Do not neglect the gift that is in you, which was given to you by prophecy with the laying on of the hands of the eldership. (1 Timothy 4:14 NKJV)

Investigate for yourself. The Scriptures mentioned in this book should give you great insight on the experience you have of the Holy Spirit and the effects that experience has on your life. Be open and receive.

HOW LONG DO THESE GIFTS LAST?

The Holy Spirit gifts don't disappear; however, if His gifts are not exercised or used, their power and strength may fade. There is a chapter coming later in this book to explain how you can develop your gifts. Don't neglect or ignore God's gifts, but use them diligently and faithfully.

For the gifts and the calling of God are irrevocable. (Romans 11:29 NKJV)

Receiving from the Holy Spirit is really an ongoing experience. Just as it can fade, it can increase and develop. You can also be renewed after experiencing a fade. God is always changing us into being more like Jesus, and it is never too late to invest in the gifts God gives you.

But when the kindness and the love of God our Savior toward man appeared, not by works of righteousness which we have done, but according to His mercy He saved us, through the washing of regeneration and renewing of the Holy Spirit, whom He poured out on us abundantly through Jesus Christ our Savior, that having been justified by His grace we should become heirs according to the hope of eternal life. (Titus 3:4–7 NKJV)

The gifts from God and His Holy Spirit are meant for everyone. There are absolutely no restrictions. Everyone can receive; but you must have experienced salvation.

"Do I qualify to receive such valuable tools from God? We are witnesses of these things, and so is the Holy Spirit, whom God freely gives to all who believe in him." (Acts 5:32 TPT)

While Peter was speaking, the Holy Spirit cascaded over all those listening to his message. The Jewish brothers who had accompanied Peter were astounded that the gift of the Holy Spirit was poured out on people who weren't Jews. (Acts 10:44–45 TPT)

So I concluded that if God is pleased to give them the same gift of the Holy Spirit that he gave us after they believed in the Lord Jesus Christ, who am I to stand in the way of God? (Acts 11:17 TPT)

ANSWERS TO COMMON QUESTIONS

Many wonder whom God's gifts are intended to benefit. His wonderful gifts can bless everyone. Yes, you can use them for your needs and those of your family, but their basic function is to benefit others. In particular, these gifts often draw the unsaved to the cross.

Each believer is given continuous revelation by the Holy Spirit to benefit not just himself but all. (1 Corinthians 12:7 TPT)

Some are also concerned about whether they will be able to control the gift of tongues. Holy Spirit is a gentleman and won't embarrass anyone by forcing them to speak in tongues. You control your tongue and when you want to speak. You will make your own decision when to allow Him to speak through you. Most enjoy it so much that they freely allow God to speak His mysteries through them. Let me know what happens to you.

The spirits of the prophets are subject to the prophets. (1 Corinthians 14:32 TPT)

What most people need to hear and understand about the gifts is that *they work through love*. As you reach out to others with God's love flowing through you, God can reach others with His supernatural healing, power, love, and everything else He has for them. You are simply a conduit. Walk, talk, and work with His love as your ultimate motivation. You will be amazed at what He can do through you.

> And if I were to have the gift of prophecy with a profound understanding of God's hidden secrets, and if I possessed unending supernatural knowledge, and if I had the greatest gift of faith that could move mountains, but have never learned to love, then I am nothing. (1 Corinthians 13:2 TPT)

The Holy Spirit continues to give a variety of gifts, but not every believer receives the same gifts. Everyone receives what they need at the moment they need it. Part of the reason for this book is to help you discover what gifts God has for you.

Are you getting excited? I am. I want you to experience everything God has planned for you. To do that, you need everything He has waiting for you.

> It is the same Holy Spirit who continues to distribute many different varieties of gifts. (1 Corinthians 12:4 TPT)

The special gifts we are discussing here are from God's Holy Spirit. After your Holy Spirit baptism, the gifts are available to operate through you. They must be received, however, and allowed to work through you. This means you have control of what flows from God through you to the person you are ministering to. By the way, these gifts also minister directly to you. This operation is explained in I Corinthians 14:23–32. I advise you to read these verses with an open heart and hear God's voice of loving instruction.

Gifts are given as a stewardship—not for personal benefit. Take a moment and read Matthew 25:14–30. This is the parable about financial stewardship. As His servants and children, we are accountable to God for how we use what He gives us.

We are given the responsibility to use these gifts for God's purposes. As you read the parable, note the fate of the person who did not use his talents wisely (see Matthew 25:18, 30). Surely, we want to take rightful joy in what God gives us, and we also want to use them to fulfill God's purpose in giving them to us.

WHAT GIFTS WILL YOU RECEIVE?

Each Spirit-filled believer should have at least one gift. They can function, however, under the operation of all nine gifts as necessary. For example, you may have the gift of tongues, but someone who needs healing is standing in front of you for ministry. Do you ignore them because you have never ministered healing before? Of course not!

You will spiritually plug into God's Holy Spirit, and He will give you the tools you need at that moment. If the person needs healing from a disease, you will pray healing over them. If they need deliverance, you will speak deliverance and then healing. This is where discernment comes into play. God's discernment working through you will activate what action is needed in a particular situation. You just have to pray to be sensitive to His voice and His Holy Spirit.

> Each believer is given continuous revelation by the Holy Spirit to benefit not just himself but all. For example: The Spirit gives to one the gift of the word of wisdom. To another, the same Spirit gives the gift of the word of revelation knowledge. And to another, the same Spirit gives the gift of faith. And to another, the same Spirit gives gifts of healing. And to another the power to work miracles. And to another the gift of prophecy. And to another the gift to discern what the Spirit is speaking. And to another the gift of speaking different kinds of tongues. And to another the gift of interpretation of tongues. Remember, it is the same Holy Spirit who distributes, activates, and operates these different gifts as he chooses for each believer. (1 Corinthians12:7–11 TPT)

IMPARTATION OF GIFTS

There is one special category we need to cover regarding how we might receive gifts from the Holy Spirit. Gifts can be and are imparted from one believer to another.

> "For I long to see you, that I may impart to you some spiritual gift, so that you may be established." (Romans 1:11 NKJV)

"Do not neglect the gift that is in you, which was given to you by prophecy with the laying on of the hands of the eldership." (1 Tim. 4:14 NKJV)

"Therefore I remind you to stir up the gift of God which is in you through the laying on of my hands." (2 Timothy 1:6 NKJV)

How does this work? Sometimes it can work simply by being around the gifts as someone is operating in them. By observing someone using the gifts, you will learn much about what God has already given you.

For example, if you are in a meeting with ministry going on, watch and learn. During my meetings, you may see any or all of the gifts being used, but I don't announce which one is in operation at the time. I pray for healing on a daily basis wherever I encounter a need. A word of prophecy may come forth spontaneously. Faith is always in operation at all times. Again, I say, watch and learn. Stay around people who operate in the gifts. Read books by authors qualified to write on the subject.

Also, I can pray that you will receive the gifts from the Holy Spirit, but God is the one who ultimately decides who receives what gifts. When God does give someone a gift by the laying on of hands by someone who already has that gift, that is called "impartation." It is perhaps one of the most important ways God has given to His body for strengthening and empowering the saints.

Then God added his witness to theirs. He validated their ministry with signs, astonishing wonders, all kinds of powerful miracles, and by the gifts of the Holy Spirit, which he distributed as he desired. (Hebrews 2:4 TPT)

"But one and the same Spirit works all these things, distributing to each one individually as He wills... But now God has set the members, each one of them, in the body just as He pleased." (1 Corinthians 12:11, 18 NKJV)

GOD IS NOT LIMITED

These are just a few of the ways God can give gifts to whomever He wishes. Just one other example is that I often ask God to anoint the hands of pastors and to give them the gifts of the Spirit.

All that I have written here are the most common ways I have seen God work, but God works in many ways. Never put Him in a box by expecting Him to do things the same way for every person or every instance of ministry.

But most of all, *ask and receive*! Pause right now to do it. Ask Holy Spirit to baptize you, or if you have already received His baptism then ask Him to fill you afresh. Open your heart and mind to Him, give Him room to work, and expect great things as God Himself comes to fill you to overflowing!

Then, taking a deep breath, he blew on them and said, "Receive the Holy Spirit." (John 20:22 TPT)

And we articulate these realities with the words imparted to us by the Spirit and not with the words taught by human wisdom. We join together Spirit-revealed truths with Spirit-revealed words. Someone living on an entirely human level rejects the revelations of God's Spirit, for they make no sense to him. He can't understand the revelations of the Spirit because they are only discovered by the illumination of the Spirit. (1 Corinthians 2:13–14 TPT)

thoughts to ponder

* What wonderful gifts have you received from God without ever asking for them?

* What prayers has He answered that changed your life?

* Which of God's promises have you believed and stood on?

* What good things do you believe God has waiting for you?

* Have you received the baptism of the Holy Spirit?

* How has this marvelous experience changed your life?

* What do you want to learn from the Holy Spirit in the future?

chapter 3

RECEIVE
GOD'S BEST

Besides the stories of Jesus and your baptism, learning about the gifts of the Holy Spirit is the most exciting thing in Scripture. This is because every believer in every church needs His help to fulfill the Great Commission, and the gifts are an immense portion of how He helps us.

The main purpose of the specific gifts of the Spirit is for the Church to function as the Body of Christ through the operation of these gifts. We have record of Jesus exercising seven of the nine gifts during His years of ministry. As we are His body, we have the ability to use all the gifts that are available from God. Our first assignment is to learn to receive what God wants to give His Body.

Remember: God is Spirit. The Holy Spirit is God's Spirit. As humans created by God, we are also spirit. The person who operates in the gifts of the Spirit is a channel from God's Spirit to the spirit of someone who has a need. The gifts of the Spirit are designed to meet the needs of people. Some manifestations will also help people know Jesus and prepare them for Heaven.

Humans operate in a physical body here on earth with minds to think and communicate with one another. I could say, "Look at that big red apple." Using your imagination, you would envision a big red apple. That's human communication.

The Spirit of God wants to communicate with the spirit of man, and the best tool for this purpose is the operation of the gifts of the Holy Spirit flowing from God through a human vessel. You are a vessel, just as I am. To operate in the gifts, you must see yourself as the vessel God is using to reach somebody else.

Our mission in this is the evangelization of the entire world:

"And he said unto them, Go ye into all the world, and preach the gospel to every creature. He that believeth and is baptized shall be saved; but he that believeth not shall be damned. And these signs shall follow them that believe; in my name shall they cast out devils; they shall speak with new tongues; they shall take up serpents; and if they drink any deadly thing, it shall not hurt them; they shall lay hands on the sick, and they shall recover." (Mark 16:15–18 KJV)

If we are to obey the Great Commission of Jesus, we must be empowered to fulfill His orders. Through the Holy Spirit and His gifts, we are equipped to follow God's plans for our lives. We are blessed with His tools to complete His vision. We know the Holy Spirit is present and active by the evidence of His gifts.

Gifts are manifested through God's chosen people. Are you chosen? I am. If you are a Christian, you are a member of His chosen.

GOD'S PROPHETIC PROMISE

As you already read in chapters 1 and 2, God has never hidden His Holy Spirit, but I yearn for you to truly understand the depth of God's promise to us regarding His Spirit. Sometimes the best thing we can do to take this truth to the place inside us it needs to reach is to simply meditate on God's Word, so I'm only going to comment on the passages you are about to read. I will simply draw out one specific promise each of these passages gives us about the Holy Spirit.

What I want you to do as you read this section is to slow down. Personalize each promise for yourself with the declaration I give you for each promise. Make these declarations out loud. This is God's Word; it is His promise to you and His desire for you, so receive it today!

"And it shall come to pass afterward that I will pour out My Spirit on all flesh; your sons and your daughters shall prophesy, your old men shall dream dreams, your young men shall see visions. And also on My menservants and on My maidservants I will pour out My Spirit in those days. And I will show wonders in the heavens and in the earth: Blood and fire and pillars of smoke. The sun shall be turned into darkness, and the moon into blood, before the coming of the great and awesome day of the Lord. And it shall come to pass that whoever calls on the name of the Lord shall be saved. For in Mount Zion and in Jerusalem there shall be deliverance, as the Lord has said, among the remnant whom the Lord calls. (Joel 2:28–32 NKJV)

Peter declared that the Spirit falling on the day of Pentecost fulfilled this prophecy from the book of Joel. It was a moment when God declared *all flesh* could receive His Holy Spirit. They could all prophesy, dream dreams, and receive visions. Social status, age, and gender made no difference—anyone could receive the Holy Spirit!

Declare: *I am part of "all flesh," therefore I can receive the Holy Spirit, prophesy, dream dreams, and see visions!*

Jesus replied, "Loving me empowers you to obey my word. And my Father will love you so deeply that we will come to you and make you our dwelling place. But those who don't love me will not obey my words. The Father did not send me to speak my own revelation, but the words of my Father. I am telling you this while I am still with you. But when the Father sends the Spirit of Holiness, the One like me who sets you free, he will teach you all things in my name. And he will inspire you to remember every word that I've told you. I leave the gift of peace with you—my peace. Not the kind of fragile peace given by the world, but my perfect peace. Don't yield to fear or be troubled in your hearts—instead, be courageous!" (John 14: 23–27 TPT)

Jesus spoke these words hours before He gave His life on the cross. He was giving His disciples a brief glimpse into the life that awaited them on the other side of that ordeal. In other words, He was describing the life He offers to us now. In this life, the Father gives us His Holy Spirit to speak to us, and the fruit of His words is peace and courage!

Declare: *Because of Jesus' promise, the Father has given me the Holy Spirit, I hear His words, and they give me peace and courage.*

Don't you realize that together you have become God's inner sanctuary and that the Spirit of God makes his permanent home in you? (1 Corinthians 3:16 TPT)

There is little I can say about this because it is already so clear but stop and really consider that God Himself lives inside you.

Declare: *God Himself lives inside me; I have become His permanent home!*

Have you forgotten that your body is now the sacred temple of the Spirit of Holiness, who lives in you? You don't belong to yourself any longer, for the gift of God, the Holy Spirit, lives inside your sanctuary. You were God's expensive purchase, paid for with tears of blood, so by all means, then, use your body to bring glory to God! (1 Corinthians 6:19–20 TPT)

Paul nails us with a sobering truth here: we don't belong to ourselves anymore. We are not merely a place God inhabits, but we are the home He owns, having purchased us with His blood. It is our responsibility, then, to live for His glory by the power of the Holy Spirit.

Declare: *God purchased my body and my life, so I will live for His purposes unto His glory.*

> The human body has many parts, but the many parts make up one whole body. So it is with the body of Christ. Some of us are Jews, some are Gentiles, some are slaves, and some are free. But we have all been baptized into one body by one Spirit, and we all share the same Spirit. Yes, the body has many different parts, not just one part… All of you together are Christ's body, and each of you is a part of it. (1 Corinthians 12:12–14, 27 NLT)

We are all separate parts of God's body. This means two wonderful things at the same time. First, life is never all about me, you, or any other believer. No matter how gifted we are, we are still only a part. Second, no matter how new we are in the body, how small we feel our gifts are, or how unimportant we think we are, we are a part of God's body. That means we are essential, not just important.

Declare: *I am one of the many parts of God's body. This means I am necessary and serve a vital purpose!*

> [The Holy Spirit] is given to us like an engagement ring, as the first installment of what's coming! He is our hope-promise of a future inheritance which seals

us until we have all of redemption's promises and experience complete freedom—all for the supreme glory and honor of God! (Ephesians 1:14 TPT)

The wildest stories you've heard of what the Holy Spirit has done in a person's life are only a foretaste of what God has in store for us in eternity. God is beginning something in you right now, today, and it is the sign to you of His promise that one day He will fully complete all His promises in you.

Declare: *God has given me His Holy Spirit so that I can be sure of His promise to fulfill all good things in my life*!

You are so passionate about embracing the manifestations of the Holy Spirit! Now become even more passionate about the things that strengthen the entire church. (1 Corinthians 14:12 TPT)

This is one of Paul's important reminders about God's heart for the gifts He gives us. While the gifts may not be primarily about us, God shows us here that each of us is well able to strengthen those around us. Considering how many Christians often feel powerless to help people, this is a truth we must feed on until we know it confidently.

Declare: *Because of the gifts God has given me, I am able to strengthen those around me with the divine power of God*!

The mature children of God are those who are moved by the impulses of the Holy Spirit. (Romans 8:14 TPT)

This is what God invites you to—living your life guided by the gentle impulses of the Spirit. He wants you to know His touch and His voice so intimately that even a whisper can direct your steps.

Declare: *I am on a path to know God intimately, to be filled with Him fully, and to be guided by even His gentlest touch for His glory.*

Meanwhile, the moment we get tired in the waiting, God's Spirit is right alongside helping us along. If we don't know how or what to pray, it doesn't matter. He does our praying in and for us, making prayer out of our wordless sighs, our aching groans. He knows us far better than we know ourselves, knows our pregnant condition, and keeps us present before God. That's why we can be so sure that every detail in our lives of love for God is worked into something good. (Romans 8:27–28 MSG)

Walking with the Holy Spirit and having His gifts does not promise us an easy life, but it does promise us help even in the moments when we feel so pressed that we have no more words. Without the Holy Spirit to understand our groans and sighs, who could help us? How could we ever find deliverance from our troubles if He weren't with us? What a comfort to know we are never alone!

Declare: *The Holy Spirit is always with me, even in my troubles, so that I will always have the help I need.*

ARE YOU READY?

With all these promises, you can see how a very active life in the Holy Spirit is God's best for us. It's like how cake is not its best until the frosting is spread over the top. I believe the Holy Spirit baptism is the same. You can enjoy the cake (salvation), but nothing is like that sweet covering that brings all the flavor to culmination on your tongue. Are you prepared for the ultimate experience?

What you once understood about this experience may change. There have been many teachings in the past about the baptism in the Holy Spirit. Some are accurate, some are partially true, and others are totally wrong.

It's time to pray and allow God to lead you. Study the Scriptures and pray about what His Word is saying to you. Let God speak to your heart.

This book is designed to stimulate your interest to develop spiritually, to clear up what the gifts are and are not, and to open your heart to grow into the leadership position God has waiting for you. You may not desire to travel the world speaking to thousands in a leadership position. You can, however, certainly be the best leader you can be within your home and with your family and friends. Just be open to what God has for you.

God is still using the operation of the gifts of the Spirit to communicate messages to mankind. These messages may be in the form of healing, edifying, exhortation, or comfort. They may also be in the form of deliverance or supplying provision. God will communicate to the person who is in need using words or actions they will understand.

He still does this through ordinary people like you and me. Through the assignment of these gifts, we can communicate God's message to somebody else. God works with and ministers through people—His children.

Some people think, "God couldn't use me because I'm just normal, a nobody. I'm not anything special."

Yes, you are special. You are created in the image of God. If God is special, then you are special. He created you with a special purpose and destiny in mind (see Jeremiah 29:11.). Part of that purpose and destiny is for God to work through you to release His power to those in need.

For example, if you had arthritis and came to me for ministry, I would command that spirit of arthritis to come out. You would be delivered from arthritic pain. What communication took place? The Spirit of God wanted to demonstrate Himself as healer working through an obedient vessel. The virtue (the *dunamis* power of God) traveled through me to you and healed your pain.

In a similar sense, if God wants you to share a word of prophecy or a word of wisdom, He will speak to your spirit. Your soul speaks to your mind and will tell you what to say. The communication from your spirit to your mouth will present some sign or information that another person will recognize.

The flow is from the Spirit of God to your spirit, into your mind, out of your mouth, and into the mind or body of the person you are ministering to. Ultimately, the message from God reaches their soul and spirit.

God is more interested in a person's spirit than their body.

Of course, God is interested in our bodies because Jesus lives within us; but He is more interested in saving our eternal souls to get us into heaven. If you are filled with the Spirit of God, then you are tuned in to God. God is able to use you in significant, eternal ways to guide people into heaven. That is His primary goal and most important message—the Gospel—and you are called to be His messenger, delivering the Gospel with power to those who need to receive it.

KNOW GOD'S VOICE

My purpose in writing this to you is much the same as Paul's purpose in writing to the Corinthians. I don't want you to be ignorant of the gifts! As Paul wrote:

> Now concerning spiritual gifts, brethren, I do not want you to be ignorant: You know that you were Gentiles, carried away to these dumb idols, however you were led. Therefore I make known to you that no one speaking by the Spirit of God calls Jesus accursed, and no one can say that Jesus is Lord except by the Holy Spirit. (1 Corinthians 12:1–3 NKJV)

I will caution you that there are wolves in sheep's clothing out there. These people appear to be working for and serving God, but they are busy misleading God's children. You will learn more about discernment in chapter 4. Pray and listen to the Holy Spirit about those you listen to.

As that verse says, "No one can say, 'Jesus is Lord,' except by the Holy Spirit." If someone doesn't have the Spirit of Christ in them, they are not a Christian (see Romans 8). With the Spirit of God working through you, you can speak forth the truth of God. Otherwise, you are speaking forth the things of this earth and the things of man.

Don't be shortchanged by opinions or suppositions. Receive all that God wants to bestow upon you. Be open and receive!

THE HOLY SPIRIT IS OUR TEACHER

There is no need to be concerned as you press into the Lord to grow in your gifts. Just keep seeking the Lord and the Holy Spirit Himself will be your teacher:

> But the Helper, the Holy Spirit, whom the Father will send in My name, He will teach you all things, and bring to your remembrance all things that I said to you. (John 14:26 NKJV)

Have you asked God for His Holy Spirit to fill your life? I think it is time to do that right now. Pray this out loud with me:

> Father, I believe in Jesus and have asked Him into my heart. I now know that Your Holy Spirit lives in me also through Jesus Christ. Father, I sincerely want everything that You have for me. I need Your help in doing everything You have planned for my future. Please baptize me with Your Holy Spirit with evidence of speaking in tongues. I promise to learn more about

You and Your Holy Spirit so I can be more like Your Son, Jesus Christ, as I minister to others in my world. I thank You for all You have done, Father. In Jesus' precious name, Amen.

thoughts to ponder

* What have you heard about the Holy Spirit in the past and how has that affected your ability to receive from Him today?

* What hindrances do you see in your life that keep you from receiving God's best through the Holy Spirit?

* What is the purpose of God's gifts?

* What does the word *evangelize* mean to you?

* What do you feel is your responsibility to follow the Great Commission, whether or not you choose to travel the world?

* What do you believe God has called you to do?

* What have you learned and experienced that you know God wants you to share with others?

chapter 4

INTRODUCING THE
GIFTS OF THE SPIRIT

Right now, I want you to take off any limits you may have when you think about the Holy Spirit. He is God's very own Spirit, and He can and does do so much more than just the one or two most well-known gifts.

> But when the truth-giving Spirit comes, he will unveil the reality of every truth within you. He won't speak on his own, but only what he hears from the Father, and he will reveal prophetically to you what is to come. (John 16:13 TPT)

Often people believe that speaking in tongues is the only or most important of the gifts from the Holy Spirit. It is important, yes, but the gifts incorporate so much more than just speaking in tongues or having a special prayer language.

There is a discussion amongst Christians about the number

of Holy Spirit gifts. We will start with the nine gifts listed in 1 Corinthians 12 and follow up in another chapter with the other gifts that God makes available to His children.

The nine gifts of the Spirit fall into three general classifications: Three *revelation gifts*—word of wisdom, word of knowledge, and discerning of spirits; three *power gifts*—faith, gift of healing, and working of miracles; and three *inspiration gifts*—prophecy, speaking in tongues (languages) you didn't learn or study, and interpretation of tongues. In this chapter, I will discuss the three revelation gifts and the three power gifts. Then in the following chapter, I will discuss the three inspiration gifts.

> Now to each one the manifestation of the Spirit is given for the common good. To one there is given through the Spirit a message of wisdom, to another a message of knowledge by means of the same Spirit, to another faith by the same Spirit, to another gifts of healing by that one Spirit, to another miraculous powers, to another prophecy, to another distinguishing between spirits, to another speaking in different kinds of tongues, and to still another the interpretation of tongues. All these are the work of one and the same Spirit, and he distributes them to each one, just as he determines. (1 Corinthians 12:7–11 TPT)

WORD OF WISDOM

A word of wisdom is a supernatural gift. It operates differently than a word of knowledge, but they are usually in agreement.

A word of wisdom finds the best way to approach a situation that would otherwise be ignored or overlooked. These ways are quite often very unique.

This is knowing something not disclosed by human knowledge, but information given by God to man through the wisdom of the Holy Spirit. This gift is often used in ministering physical and inner healing.

Words of wisdom create an atmosphere of peace when they are released. They produce a clear sense that God is acting in a special way which removes any spirit of fear or anxiety that otherwise fills the people in that moment. Those involved know what they should be doing and have a newfound faith that God is acting or will act on their behalf.

Don't you know that I'm ready to pour out my spirit of wisdom upon you and bring to you the revelation of my words that will make your heart wise? (Proverbs 1:23 TPT)

And if anyone longs to be wise, ask God for wisdom and he will give it! He won't see your lack of wisdom as an opportunity to scold you over your failures but he will overwhelm your failures with his generous grace. (James 1:5 TPT)

We see this gift working even in the Old Testament during the life of Solomon (remember, the Holy Spirit has always been at work?). One instance illustrates this gift especially well.

Two women came to Solomon for justice. They lived in the

same house, both had babies, but one of the babies had died at night. Now they were fighting over the one living baby, both claiming it as their own.

How could Solomon know which was the true mother of the baby? They had no DNA testing then, so he needed a word of wisdom.

"Take a sword and cut the baby in half," he declared. This shows just how unusual God's words of wisdom might sometimes sound, but we will see he had no intention of killing the child.

As a guard brought forward a sword to obey his king, one of the women said, "Fine, he won't be yours or mine," but the other woman said, "No! Give her the child, but just let him live!"

"Stop!" Solomon commanded, and he ordered the baby to be given to the woman who had pleaded for the child's life. Her cry for his life above all else had proven she was his true mother.

That is God's wisdom at work through the gift of word of wisdom (see more of this story in 1 Kings 3:16–28).

WORD OF KNOWLEDGE

When you are in prayer or worship, you may suddenly have a thought that allows you to know things that you could not ordinarily know. It could be any kind of knowledge, but usually it is information about a person or group of people and their divine calling from God. It could contain a word of direction or a word of warning. At other times a word of knowledge may consist of just one word, literally one word and nothing else. This may mean nothing to the person receiving it, but a great deal to someone else in the meeting.

At other times the word of knowledge may be a picture or an image of something. Over time one learns how to use words of knowledge intelligently and wisely. A word of knowledge often releases energy and a sense of hope into the people involved. Again, this could be meaningful to just one person in the meeting, several people present or those watching a meeting streaming online or by video.

Occasionally, a musician may choose a particular song to start a service. Without communicating with the speaker, the song and topic of the message for the day line up perfectly. The Holy Spirit communicated God's will to the people involved. I consider that a word of knowledge.

DISCERNING OF SPIRITS

The discerning of spirits is one of the most important of the spiritual gifts because it provides a defense against the attacks of the enemy, while giving insight into the many and diverse effects evil spirits have on people, buildings, and nations. This gift provides believers with tools they can use to walk in victory over evil and help others do the same.

This gift can help you know the presence of the Holy Spirit and recognize the anointing and voice of His Holy Spirit talking to your spirit. Listen for His voice and obey. He will protect you and direct your actions. His guidance is vital to survival while negotiating this world's confusion and distractions.

It can also help you know the presence of evil spirits. Pay attention to the uneasiness you feel around certain situations or people. God's Spirit is warning you of the spirit living within the people nearby or what has happened previously in that environment. Enter into a church where God has been worshipped and you will be surrounded with peace, but nearing a person or place where Satan is worshipped makes you feel like you need to run...*fast*! This uncomfortable uneasiness or awareness may save your life—spiritually and physically.

If this uneasiness occurs when you are ministering to someone, ask another believer to minister with you. It is best to minister in pairs, just like Jesus instructed His disciples to do.

Discerning of spirits can help you know when a gift of the spirit is in the flesh or is from God. There are many false prophets working in the world. That fact is scriptural (see Matthew 7:15–23). The enemy takes something beautiful from God's creation and uses it for his agenda. Music of the world is a prime example. God created beautiful music filled with peace, love, and joy, but the enemy has his counterfeit music which promotes discontent, immorality, hate, and pain.

You can also use this gift to recognize a person who claims to be a Christian when evidence is not present. When you are exposed to unfamiliar people, whether at a meeting or on television, you must learn to test their spirit. Are they speaking the truth of the Word of God or twisting His words to fit their agenda? The Holy Spirit can reveal whether the person's spirit is in conflict with God. Test the spirit.

Ask the Holy Spirit for guidance. Study God's Word. Research the speaker's background and history. Seek advice from a trusted leader before you accept and repeat a questionable teaching. Is the person walking in the peace, joy, and love of the Holy Spirit? Or is their charismatic personality dotted with questionable words or behavior?

Discernment can also help you know whether or not advice or prophecy given to you is from God. If a word or teaching doesn't line up with the Word of God, my advice is to consult with a trusted mentor. Don't just accept a word of prophecy and immediately change your life or direction. There is usually confirmation from other directions if the message is truly from God.

Another ministry that commonly uses discernment of spirits is deliverance ministry. There is almost always a reason someone has a demon, and discernment can help you identify the root issue based on what kind of spirit came to afflict a person. If it is a spirit of lust, anger, deception, manipulation, or some other sin, you can lead the person in repentance from that sin. If it is a spirit of trauma or fear, you can lead the person to receive healing from the original hurt they are still held captive to because of the spirit at work in their lives. Ultimately, it is our authority in Christ that compels demons to leave, but guiding afflicted people through this process helps them stay free from demonic affliction.

Different gifts often work together in ministry, including deliverance ministry. For example, a word of knowledge and discerning of spirits often work together. When ministering to someone, you must know (or discern) whether a spirit must be cast out or when a healing is required. The former requires casting out a spirit; the latter calls for a healing.

When Jesus saw that the people came running together, He rebuked the unclean spirit, saying to it,

"Deaf and dumb spirit, I command you, come out of him and enter him no more!" Then the spirit cried out, convulsed him greatly, and came out of him. And he became as one dead, so that many said, "He is dead." But Jesus took him by the hand and lifted him up, and he arose. (Mark 9:25–27 NKJV)

Some people brought to him a deaf man with a severe speech impediment. They pleaded with Jesus to place his hands on him and heal him. So Jesus led him away from the crowd to a private spot. Then he stuck his fingers into the man's ears and placed some of his saliva on the man's tongue. Then he gazed into heaven, sighed deeply, and spoke to the man's ears and tongue, "Ethpathakh," which is Aramaic for "Open up, now!" (Mark 7:32–34 TPT)

FAITH

God blesses us all with a specific amount of faith. Some people claim to have no faith, yet every baby learns faith very early through such things as faith that their mom and dad will come when they cry. We learn that a chair is safe to sit on or a car will run when we use a key. When we flip a light switch, we have faith that the lights will come on or turn off. Pick up your phone and you have faith that you can reach your loved ones or associates for a chat or meeting. Many people don't realize they are living and functioning with a measure of faith in their environment with every minute of life.

Let me ask you again: What does the lavish supply of the Holy Spirit in your life and the miracles of God's tremendous power have to do with you keeping religious laws? The Holy Spirit is poured out upon us through the revelation and power of faith! (Galatians 3:5 TPT)

God sometimes releases a supernatural anointing for faith. While it lingers, a person has a sense that God can and will do whatever they ask God to do. Miracles will be abundant in this atmosphere of faith. Amazing phenomena can occur, too. This can include healings; signs and wonders; financial provision; food multiplying; deliverance from accidents, diseases, or physical attacks; and more.

It is also true that God sometimes raises up individuals with a unique gift for faith in almost any situation. They bring an atmosphere of victory with them that is contagious and full of wonder. Occasionally, I meet someone who manifests very little faith that God can do anything for them. My reply to their words of doubt is, "I believe I have enough faith for both of us. I know what my God can do!"

We look away from the natural realm and we focus our attention and expectation onto Jesus who birthed faith within us and who leads us forward into faith's perfection. His example is this: Because his heart was focused on the joy of knowing that you would be his, he endured the agony of the cross and conquered its humiliation, and now sits exalted at the right hand of the throne of God! (Hebrews 12:2 TPT)

Faith is believing not just with your mind, but with your heart and spirit. You will believe God and His promises, which are activated as you exercise this belief. Faith combined with hope becomes substance. Be sensitive to what God tells you to do, then *do it*. You have all the faith you need if you have faith to hear God's voice.

Faith, then, is birthed in a heart that responds to God's anointed utterance of the Anointed One. (Romans 10:17 TPT)

Faith cannot be attained by our efforts—it is a gift. Faith can be developed as it is exercised for daily or special miracles as we show that we really do trust God for humanly impossible acts.

There is no way for me to fully cover the subject of faith in this brief section, so I encourage you to study this more for yourself. A great place to start is by reading Hebrews 11 and asking the Holy Spirit to open your spirit to what He has for you.

HEALING

The gift of healing is a divine anointing to perform supernatural miracles of bodily reconstruction, disease resolution, and pain relief. It also opens the door for many to receive the Gospel and be saved. Healing evangelists equip the body of Christ to perform miracles themselves and lead many into salvation as God's Holy Spirit gifts are manifested.

Any born-again believer can minister or pray for healing, but not all are equally gifted. A believer must learn how to develop their gift. The most important element in developing any gift of the Spirit is persistence. Many people simply determined by faith that they would see miracles, so they prayed for every person they saw who needed one. Sometimes they saw no miracles, even after praying for a hundred people, but as they persisted in faith and obedience, God grew their gift until they became powerful healing ministers.

Obedience is often a key to healing miracles. Jesus and the disciples generally told the person being healed to do something, and as they obeyed, they were healed. Here are just a few of the many examples:

Then He said to the man, "Stretch out your hand." And he stretched it out, and it was restored as whole as the other. (Matthew 12:13 NKJV)

Then Jesus spat on the ground and made some clay with his saliva. Then he anointed the blind man's eyes with the clay. And he said to the blind man, "Now go and wash the clay from your eyes in the ritual pool of Siloam." So he went and washed his face and as he came back, he could see for the first time in his life! (John 9:6–7 TPT)

Jesus said to him, "Stand up! Pick up your sleeping mat and you will walk!" Immediately he stood up—he was healed! So he rolled up his mat and walked again! Now Jesus worked this miracle on the Sabbath. (John 5:8–9 TPT)

Then Peter said, "Silver and gold I do not have, but what I do have I give you: In the name of Jesus Christ of Nazareth, rise up and walk." And he took him by the right hand and lifted him up, and immediately his feet and ankle bones received strength. (Acts 3:6–7)

On his way to Jerusalem Jesus passed through the border region between Samaria and Galilee. As he entered one village, ten men approached him, but they kept their distance, for they were lepers. They shouted to him, "Mighty Lord, our wonderful Master! Won't you have mercy on us and heal us?" When Jesus stopped to look at them, he spoke these words: "Go to be examined by the Jewish priests." They set off, and they were healed while walking along the way. One of them, a Samaritan, when he discovered that he was completely healed, turned back to find Jesus, shouting out joyous praises and glorifying God. When he found Jesus, he fell down at his feet and thanked him over and over, saying to him, "You are the Messiah." "So where are the other nine?" Jesus asked. "Weren't there ten who were healed? They all refused to return to give thanks and give glory to God except you, a foreigner from Samaria?" Then Jesus said to the healed man lying at his feet, "Arise and go. It was your faith that brought you salvation and made you whole." (Luke 17:11–19 TPT)

If a demon or unclean spirit is causing an illness or infirmity, it must be cast out for the body or mind to be healed. I usually start with a prayer for healing. If nothing happens, I will go on to cast out or bind the spirit behind the infirmity. This can include spirit of death (cancer or other terminal disease), arthritis, depression, or pain, but there are many.

Jesus spoke as a man of authority when He confronted demons. We, as God's other children, must do the same. Yes, the word of wisdom and word of knowledge are in operation here, but faith is also a key component.

> "For assuredly, I say to you, whoever says to this mountain, 'Be removed and be cast into the sea,' and does not doubt in his heart, but believes that those things he says will be done, he will have whatever he says. Therefore I say to you, whatever things you ask when you pray, believe that you receive them, and you will have them." (Mark 11:23–24 NKJV)

> "You can say to this Mount of Olives, 'Rise up and fall into the Mediterranean,' and your command will be obeyed." (Mark 11:23–24 TLB)

WORKING OF MIRACLES

In some ways, one of the more interesting gifts is the gift of working of miracles. What makes it interesting is that miracles can look like so many different things.

For example, miracles can be healings, but not all healings are miracles . Healings such as where body parts are replaced or regrown are miracles. Miracles can often also be signs and wonders of various kinds. Where I see miracles the most, however, is in the form of provision.

For instance, Jesus turned the water into wine, calmed the waves, and fed the multitudes:

Mary then went to the servers and told them, "Whatever Jesus tells you, do it!"

Nearby stood six stone water pots meant to be used for the Jewish washing rituals. Each one could hold about twenty gallons or more. Jesus came to the servers and instructed them, "Fill the pots with water, right up to the very brim." Then he said, "Now fill your pitchers and take them to the master of ceremonies."

And when they poured out their pitchers for the master of ceremonies to sample, the water had become wine! When he tasted the water that had become wine, the master of ceremonies was impressed with its quality. (Although he didn't know where the wine had come from, only the servers knew.) He called the bridegroom over and said to him, "Every host serves his best wine first, until everyone has had a cup or two, then he serves the cheaper wine. But you, my friend, you've reserved the most exquisite wine until now!" (John 2: 5–10 NKJV)

For more examples of miracles Jesus worked, read: Matthew 8:26, Matthew 14:21, Matthew 16:10, and Mark 6:44.

During my years in ministry, I have experienced so many instances of miraculous provisions. You can read about many of them in my books, *Healing the Heart* and *Supernatural Provision*.

thoughts to ponder:

* What gifts would you like to work through you as you minister?

* Have you asked for these gifts? What gifts have you asked for?

* Is it hard or difficult to ask for gifts from God? Why?

* What gifts do you believe you have received?

* What gifts are the most developed and what gifts do you want to mature and grow more?

chapter 5

THE INSPIRATION GIFTS

ne of my favorite things is to see people get activated in the gifts of the Holy Spirit. You see this light come into their eyes as they realize they not only feel His presence, but they can see His explosive power work in and through them.

God never chooses anyone because they are special in the world's eyes. In fact, Paul tells the Corinthians that God intentionally chooses the people who aren't special in the world's eyes so that everyone will recognize what that person does as having been done by God's power alone (see 1 Corinthians 1:18–31). That way it continues to point people to Him so He can continue reaching more people.

I hope you are beginning to feel that light come into your eyes even by reading about the first six spiritual gifts in chapter 4. Now I'm going to talk to you about the next three gifts—the inspiration gifts: prophecy, speaking in tongues, and interpretation of tongues. These three gifts get their very own chapter because so many people often have so many questions about these. I want to clear all these questions out of your way so nothing hinders you as you learn to walk in the Spirit.

PROPHECY

The first inspiration gift is the gift of prophecy. This gift can help bring powerful transformation to people's lives. Paul says this about the purpose for prophecy:

> But when someone prophesies, he speaks to encourage people, to build them up, and to bring them comfort. (1 Corinthians 14:3 TPT)

> So then, tongues are not a sign for believers, but a miracle for unbelievers. Prophecy, on the other hand, is not for unbelievers, but a miracle sign for believers. (1 Corinthians 14:22 TPT)

> It is good that you are enthusiastic and passionate about spiritual gifts, especially prophecy. (1 Corinthians 14:1 TPT)

Prophetic words can be given in many ways: tongues and interpretation, visions and dreams, angelic visitations, words of knowledge and wisdom, as well as other modalities. Prophetic acts can also have a powerful effect, such as the Hebrews marching around Jericho until the walls of the city fell (see Joshua 6).

As a personal example, I have often had artists who painted

pictures during a meeting in which I was going to speak. These artists listen to the Holy Spirit about what they should paint, and it is incredible to see how often their paintings speak directly to a person or circumstance about which they knew nothing beforehand.

We must use wisdom when delivering prophetic words to make sure they are timely, sometimes even by praying through the word before delivering it, or it can lead to confusion. We need to remember what God tells us is the purpose of prophetic ministry: encouraging people, building them up, and bringing them comfort. It is not to show how spiritual or revelatory we are. It is not to direct someone's choices. It is not to confront sin in their lives by naming it and calling it out. It is simply so they are drawn closer to God in love and truth.

One area that caused confusion in the early church is that people would all prophesy at the same time. This was partly good, as Paul told the Corinthians that he desired that all might prophecy (see 1 Corinthians 14:5). Any believer could hear the voice of God and any believer could share that prophetic word with a congregation. This was good, but everyone competing to be heard at the same time didn't express God's love because it was confusing, not helpful, therefore Paul corrected them and reminded them what prophecy is for.

When done wisely, prophecy can change a person's life. My mom, Frances Hunter, spoke a beautiful prophecy over a lady in Oklahoma City. When God picked her out of the audience, Mom asked her to come to the front. The Holy Spirit of God spoke to the lady's spirit, but the communication had to travel through Mom's mind and voice.

The message God wanted to share with this young woman transformed her life. Above all, God wanted to minister to her spirit, not just her mind or her body. God wants to use these Holy Spirit gifts so He can minister to people.

There is a difference between giving a prophetic word and being a prophet. We will be discussing the office of a prophet in the next chapter, but a prophecy is usually a word about something that will or could happen in the future. It can be given about a person, a group of people, or a nation. The words should edify (build up), exhort (encourage), and comfort.

Preaching can often move into prophecy when the preacher is under a heavy anointing. "Personal prophecy" can be in the flesh, or in other words, it often exalts man instead of Jesus. Be careful with personal prophecy from someone you don't know anything about. It can become manipulative. Most authentic personal prophecy will be a confirmation of something God has been talking to you about already. Remember, two or more witnesses are necessary to confirm a thing.

That by the mouth of two or three witnesses every word may be established. (Matthew 18:16 TPT)

SPEAKING IN TONGUES

Prophecy and interpretation of tongues can look very similar; however, an utterance in an unknown tongue always precedes an interpretation.

Regarding speaking in tongues, when a Christian is filled or baptized with the Holy Spirit, God often gives that person a spoken language that is completely unlike any earthly tongue.

Though I speak with the tongues of men and of angels,
but have not love, I have become sounding brass or a
clanging cymbal. (I Corinthians 13:1 NKJV)

It sometimes bubbles up from within the believer and may
or may not have an obvious meaning or immediate interpretation. This is sometimes referred to as a prayer language. You
may also hear this described by the phrase, "Baptism of the
Holy Spirit with evidence of speaking in tongues."

"He who believes in Me, as the Scripture has said, out
of his heart will flow rivers of living water." (John 7:38
NKJV)

This tongue or language becomes an ongoing method for
encouraging and strengthening the speaker. It is also a means
of praying when the individual does not know how he or she
should pray.

And in a similar way, the Holy Spirit takes hold of us
in our human frailty to empower us in our weakness.
For example, at times we don't even know how to pray,
or know the best things to ask for. But the Holy Spirit
rises up within us to super-intercede on our behalf,
pleading to God with emotional sighs too deep for
words. (Romans 8:26 TPT)

For instance, you find yourself suddenly thinking about a
friend or relative. You have no idea what is going on in their

lives, but you strongly feel something is happening. You have no idea of the details, but, thankfully, you don't need to know anything more about the situation. You simply start speaking (or praying) in tongues.

When you pray in tongues, you are actually speaking God's own thoughts about the person and their situation back to Him. This is a powerful tool for building yourself up and encouraging yourself on a daily basis while also praying in a completely appropriate manner for others. You may only see a face and feel strongly to pray for that person. You aren't crazy; you are simply hearing from God that someone needs your prayers at the moment.

Years ago, a lady's daughter was kidnapped. There was no trace for the authorities to follow. The mother was frantic and had no idea what to do. God told her to go to a certain intersection on the other side of town, park her car, and pray in tongues. In obedience, she followed His instructions every day for weeks. When the case finally broke and the daughter was returned to her mother's loving arms, it was revealed that the young lady was being held in a structure twenty feet from where her mother had parked the car and prayed.

Many times, I have been nearly speechless with the situations I face and stories I hear from other people. I have learned that being speechless doesn't accomplish anything. I quickly and under my breath say, "Father, help me! Holy Spirit, give me Your words to say!" I depend on Him completely. I couldn't minister or travel around the world doing His work without His constant help.

You will learn to do the same thing. For instance, right

now, today, I am sure you know of a friend or loved one who is going through something difficult. Many have physical, mental, emotional, or financial issues they are facing. With the Holy Spirit's assistance, you don't need to know the specific details. Tell them to simply text you on their phone with the word, "Help!" or "Pray!" By praying in your Holy Spirit prayer language, you will be speaking or praying the perfect words directly to God.

Most who pray in their native language (such as English) want or need to know details so they can pray "correctly." Yes, there are times that is necessary. For instance, I want to know the problems you are facing so I can minister to you appropriately. However, you can often just pray in tongues in intercession over the situation. You may wake up in the middle of the night with a specific person on your mind. You feel something is happening, but you don't even know how or where to reach the person. Just connect with the Holy Spirit and start praying. Remember:

> For example: The Spirit gives to one the gift of the word of wisdom. To another, the same Spirit gives the gift of the word of revelation knowledge. And to another, the same Spirit gives the gift of faith. And to another, the same Spirit gives gifts of healing. And to another the power to work miracles. And to another the gift of prophecy. And to another the gift to discern what the Spirit is speaking. And to another the gift of speaking different kinds of tongues. And to another the gift of interpretation of tongues. Remember, it is

the same Holy Spirit who distributes, activates, and operates these different gifts as he chooses for each believer. (1 Corinthians 12:8–11 TPT)

Those who have received the gift of tongues can use it to whisper, speak, or sing any time they choose. Whether you are in church or lying in your bed, the Holy Spirit will give you the language to speak.

Years ago, Mom told a story. She said, "If you speak in tongues around other people (such as walking through the grocery store), someone may think you are strange (another word for crazy). However, if you sing in tongues as you are walking through the store, they may think, "Not only does that person know another language, but they sing in another language. How wonderful!"

The main reason I wanted to mention that story is that you may want or need to pray in tongues now wherever you are now. For instance, someone calls or texts you, "Pray." You don't know any details and you don't need to know any. You just start to pray (or sing) in tongues. The Holy Spirit knows the perfect words. Yes, you can "think" in tongues, but speaking in tongues is more effective.

Keep in mind, also, that you may feel led to speak or pray in tongues while other people are around you. Feel free to do so. You may be speaking in the language of someone nearby who has been praying for an answer to their own prayer. It has happened. Your "prayer language" may sound like German or Italian one day and Chinese or Russian the next. God gives you the words to speak without informing you what language you are speaking. You never know who is hearing God's message delivered through the gift of tongues.

TONGUES AS A FORM OF PROPHETIC UTTERANCE

Can *you* give a prophetic message in an unknown tongue? Yes, when the Spirit tells you to. This may happen after you have received the baptism of the Holy Spirit but could happen in any public gathering of believers as well.

Sometimes a person feels compelled by the Holy Spirit to speak loudly in tongues during a corporate gathering of Christians. They may sense that God wants the entire group to hear from Him but may not have a message to share that is understandable. The Holy Spirit inside that individual pours out in an unknown tongue and the congregation waits for God to reveal the meaning of that message through someone in the group. This gift of tongues is not the same as the prayer language you receive during the baptism of the Holy Spirit. This prophetic utterance is to encourage and instruct the body of Christ in a public meeting.

Before speaking in tongues in a public meeting, ask for permission. Make sure the organization accepts you and will not escort you out the door. Receiving permission before any spiritual utterance is best.

INTERPRETATION OF TONGUES

Also, this gift always works in conjunction with the gift of interpretation. Paul wrote to the Corinthians about this specific issue because they didn't understand how to use the gift properly. They had a room full of people all speaking in tongues at the same time, competing with each other to be heard. Paul said that this does no one any good, so it forgets the purpose of God's spiritual gifts—the common good of the body. He instructed them to each take turns, if they felt they had a word for the whole body, and to leave room for interpretation. He said that without interpretation, the words can build up the speaker, but no one else, and that it is therefore better in public to only say things everyone will understand.

> I would be delighted if you all spoke in tongues, but I desire even more that you impart prophetic revelation to others. Greater gain comes through the one who prophesies than the one who speaks in tongues, unless there is interpretation so that it builds up the entire church. (I Corinthians 14:5 TPT)

When a message is given in tongues publicly, the Christians in the meeting should therefore wait quietly for God to interpret that message through one of the members. Paul implies that when the Spirit speaks through someone in tongues, He will also interpret that word.

Recognize when God tells you to give a message. Be sensitive to the Holy Spirit's prompting. Then give that word by faith, not by knowledge.

The nature of the gift of tongues is that they are unknown languages. Sometimes someone who hears an utterance will understand the language, but that person is almost never the giver of the word.

Because you can't figure out the interpretation with your mind, simply open yourself to the Spirit. Open your mind to Him so He can give you His thoughts and understanding. The Holy Spirit will give the interpretation by vision, thought, impression, or by some other divine means.

Interpretation is not usually a direct translation. It can be developed just as a preacher would develop a full message from one or two verses in the Bible.

> Remember, it is the same Holy Spirit who distributes, activates, and operates these different gifts as he chooses for each believer. (1 Corinthians 12:10–11 TPT)

thoughts to ponder:

* What is the gift of prophecy for?

* Have you ever received a prophetic word that encouraged you? What was it?

* How much do you desire (or not desire) to give people words of encouragement through prophecy or speaking in tongues? How could this benefit those who might receive words through you?

* Besides the examples given in this chapter, what are other benefits to praying in the Spirit when you don't know what to pray?

chapter 6

EVEN MORE
GIFTS

God lavishes gifts upon His children, both to show His goodness to the one who receives the gifts and to express His love through them by supernatural power. In the last chapter, I covered the nine gifts listed in 1 Corinthians, but as I said, other passages tell us of even more gifts. One of these passages comes from Ephesians:

And he has appointed some with grace to be apostles, and some with grace to be prophets, and some with grace to be evangelists, and some with grace to be pastors, and some with grace to be teachers. And their calling is to nurture and prepare all the holy believers to do their own works of ministry, and as they do this they will enlarge and build up the body of Christ. These grace ministries will function until we all attain oneness into the faith, until we all experience the fullness of what it means to know the Son of God, and finally we become one into a perfect man with the full dimensions of spiritual maturity and fully developed into the abundance of Christ. And then our immaturity will end! And we will not be easily shaken by trouble, nor led astray by novel teachings or by the false doctrines of deceivers who teach clever lies. (Ephesians 4:11–14 TPT)

Some may not consider people as gifts, but here Paul refers to people whom God has truly given as gifts to the body of Christ. Each person whom God calls in this way has a specific assignment to fulfill on this earth. These assignments and responsibilities are not easy and must not be considered lightly. As Ephesians 4 explains, these people are necessary to perfect the saints, do the work of ministry and train the Body of Christ. Learning to follow the Great Commission requires some instruction and equipping.

These offices or assignments have also been called the "Grace Gifts." God blesses these people with His merciful and wondrous grace for the sake of imparting that grace as they minister to and equip others. These are truly gifts to the body of Christ because they enable the body to live like Christ in ways they could not otherwise.

God has placed in the church the following: First apostles, second prophets, third teachers, then those with gifts of miracles, gifts of divine healing, gifts of revelation knowledge, gifts of leadership, and gifts of different kinds of tongues. (1 Corinthians 12:28 TPT)

THE OFFICE OF AN APOSTLE

Most denominations accept and function with pastors and teachers on a regular basis. Some also recognize the office of an apostle. In general, apostles are often recognized because they have an ability to grow ministries that impact a large number of people, and this is particularly true if those ministries grow in typically hard, dry, or unreached places.

For this reason, many churches have an apostle as an overseer to church leadership and government. Apostles have also been recognized more in recent years as large churches develop branches in other areas or cities. A church pastor and the apostle overseer usually have a close relationship whether in person, by phone, or online. They build this relationship so the grace God has given the apostle can benefit the pastor, and, through the pastor, the local congregation.

It is important to note that the supernatural is almost always present in an apostle's ministry because their ultimate job is to represent heaven. Compared to earth, everything in heaven is supernatural, so you will often see miracles, signs, and wonders under an apostle's ministry.

Personally, I function in all areas mentioned in Ephesians. Sometimes, I am a pastor, often I am a teacher, I travel as an evangelist, and I prophesy. I am considered an apostle because I function in all areas of the five-fold ministry (five-fold is the name often used to refer to these five gifts). I encourage and mentor new pastors after their ordination at Joan Hunter Ministries.

THE OFFICE OF AN EVANGELIST

During special meetings, an evangelist may visit to stir up the congregation and hopefully get people saved or recommitted to Christ. An evangelist normally travels between churches. They usually have a special message that could include prophecy, healing, or other similar demonstrations of the Spirit, but an evangelist's goal is always the winning of souls.

When a developed evangelist ministers, the room will often be filled with a strong atmosphere of repentance to the point where people feel an inner compulsion to respond. I have even heard of people who have walked with God for decades feeling this compulsion to go forward during an alter call for salvation, so strong is the grace to lead people to salvation.

Not all evangelists minister publicly in this way, however. Some minister to equip everyday saints to evangelize and win souls. This is also a gift of God to the body of Christ that helps us be "fully developed into the abundance of Christ" (Ephesians 4:13 TPT).

THE OFFICE OF A PROPHET

A prophet is a person God has set aside to equip the greater body of Christ to hear His voice accurately and who is given great revelation and discernment in the spirit realm. Prophets constantly interact with pastors, teachers, evangelists, and apostles to provide guidance for the whole body of Christ.

This succinct description might seem insignificant because it's so brief but consider how different this is from the Old Testament. In those days, only a prophet could hear from God or prophesy, but in the New Testament God has given prophets to the body of Christ so that everyone can prophesy.

Because God has given prophets to the body, they can hear from God for a person, a local body of believers, or even a workplace or city (likely for the purpose of declaration or intercession). Prophets can then see the impact of their obedience as they release the word of the Lord, which then deepens their confidence that they hear God's voice, which draws them into a deeper relationship with Him.

So much good happens both in us individually and in the body as a whole because God has given us prophets who help all believers hear His voice and learn how to deliver what He says to us.

THE OFFICE OF A PASTOR

Just as not everyone in these other offices serves in a single church, not every person who works as a pastor is a five-fold pastor. That doesn't mean they are any less in any way—no less effective, skilled, or able to do their job. It most likely only means there is some difference in their calling or assignment.

Remember that the office of a prophet is a gift of God to equip the church so that *everyone* can hear God for themselves. In the same way, a five-fold pastor equips the body so everyone can shepherd those around them in a way that brings internal health, nurture, and comfort.

This is because the role of a pastor is to act as a shepherd to the flock of God. Their primary concern is with those who are already saved, to make sure they are walking "in green pastures" spiritually and protected from spiritual predators who want to shipwreck their faith.

Someone walking in this gift in a church might not be known for their teaching, but may be known for their love and care, how they reach out and comfort others, and everyone in their church feels loved.

THE OFFICE OF A TEACHER

When an anointed individual teaches the Bible, they release an atmosphere of revelation. This supernatural gift goes far beyond the usual distribution of information. When the Holy Spirit is released through divine understanding of the Bible, great things occur and lives are changed forever. This gift causes God's Word to come alive, and to move from being words and rules on a page to being the life-giving and reality-shaping word of God for each individual. This kind of teaching about God's Word and interpreting it in ways that expands knowledge in others is vital to the spread of the Good News.

You may feel the teacher "read your mail," or in other words, they may suddenly answer questions you have been pondering right in the middle of their message. Suddenly, a Bible verse you are familiar with has a new meaning in your situation. The message may have you totally captivated to the point that you can't take notes fast enough to record all the great points discussed.

If you happen to be a teacher in any natural sense, ask God for His anointing to come upon you for it. You may be teaching thousands or just one new employee. You may be teaching your child. Whatever your position, His anointing is often necessary to increase your effectiveness in imparting wisdom and knowledge to another person.

RELY ON THE HOLY SPIRIT

You may serve in the office of an apostle, a prophet, a teacher, a pastor, or an evangelist. My mom and dad were chosen to be evangelists and teachers. Along with that call, they had the gift of writing. God endowed both them and me with an ability to put forth His truth by writing books to travel where we couldn't physically reach. We write by the gift of God. God has enlightened us more in the area in which He has called us to serve. He will do the same for you as you walk in faith.

> It is the same Holy Spirit who continues to distribute many different varieties of gifts. The Lord Yahweh is one, and he is the one who apportions to believers different varieties of ministries. The same God distributes different kinds of miracles that accomplish different results through each believer's gift and ministry as he energizes and activates them. Each believer is given continuous revelation by the Holy Spirit to benefit not just himself but all. (1 Corinthians 12:4–7 TPT)

We all operate freely in a variety of gifts, but it is the same Spirit—God's Holy Spirit—who directs our steps. Meetings hosted by various Christian leaders or speakers usually will look different from one another. Each has its own personality just like the servant who sponsors the meeting. You will experience different effects from ministers with different callings and purposes, but God is fitting together His body of believers to complete and perfect the Body of Christ.

You may not ever stand behind a pulpit, or you may be chosen as the next Billy Graham. Whatever your ministry is, there will be manifestations of the Holy Spirit through you if you have experienced the baptism of the Holy Spirit. God will give you a work or a manifestation of the Holy Spirit for something specific that He wants to do through you. God will reveal your calling to you.

Keep in mind that Jesus did not minister the same to every person who had a need. He individualized His words and actions to meet the situation at hand. Yes, He spoke; but He also touched, looked, and spat on the ground to make a mud salve. Be sensitive to what God wants you to do under the direction of the Holy Spirit.

OTHER GIFTS

We can look to Scripture to introduce us to many of the gifts God makes available to His children, but even Scripture does not name every single gift God may give to His children. Our God who created the universe is also creative in His generosity toward us.

I'm sure you have known someone who was so naturally talented at something that people referred to them as "gifted." Quite often, this is actually true. God has gifted them to do what they do and make it look so effortless.

Consider the effect those people have on those around them

when they use those gifts. It brings life. It relieves others of the burden of trying to do something they are not able to do well. It creates atmospheres of peace where healing can happen. In fact, it does so many things that it's hard to list it all, but I want to name just a few more gifts of the Spirit for you. As you read these, listen for the Spirit's prompting for where He has gifted you, then ask Him how you can steward that gift in your life.

HOSPITALITY AND HELPS

Sometimes we overlook special gifts such as helps and hospitality. They may seem natural and earthly in nature on the surface, but they are totally supernatural. Those who do not possess these gifts may describe their frustration at any attempt to copy those who so easily bless others with their hospitality gift.

God is able to use these people to do what some view as mundane chores in such a manner that lives are changed and joy is released. They are able to achieve more with less than other people and they leave a sense of contentment and peace wherever they have been.

If you love to welcome people and serve them with love and joy, you probably have this gift. Helping others is very rewarding and you probably see or know what others need without anyone telling you. This is truly a gift of the Holy Spirit.

ART AND MUSIC

Artists and musicians anointed by the Holy Spirit can produce songs and art that have a powerful effect on people for many generations. Both forms of beauty release a supernatural sense of God's love and power that can change lives and lead others to God. This is not entertainment, but worship and sacrifice. When it is a Spirit-led work, both activities glorify God and cause men to seek Him.

If you ever have the opportunity to watch an artist at work during an anointed worship or teaching service, you will never forget it. Just like God speaks through verbal communication, God works through their hands as gorgeous paintings are created within a short period of time.

The whole book of Psalms is an example of this, as is the biblical Temple, filled with images of various plants and cherubim worked into the golden walls. These works of art obviously led people to worship God and were created by gifted people under the anointing of the Holy Spirit.

Nearly everyone enjoys music. Once you have been in the presence of anointed music, you will easily know the difference between earthly noise and music ordained by God. Music is intimately connected to our emotional and spiritual health.

God's creations are heavenly and bring peace, love, joy, and healing. The music of the world causes agitation, irritation, and disquiet, or stirs people to long for things that are against the best God's wisdom and love desires for us. The next time you hear music of any kind, ask yourself how it makes you feel.

A friend of mine played Christian music in her home 24/7. It was very subtle and quiet, but its peace and anointing filled the house. People coming into her home would often say, "Your home is so peaceful!"

If your home has any stress, confusion, or agitation, my advice is to play Christian music. The anointing can consume the atmosphere and ease the negativity of the home and/or people living there. The music can be played very quietly somewhere in the home; it doesn't have to be loud to be effective. If you are alone, turn up the volume to your comfort level and enjoy!

GIVING AND ACTS OF CHARITY

Some Christians have mastered the art of joyous giving and are a continual source of help for those in need. This is not burdensome to them at all, but rather a series of loving acts that never grows old. They light the way for other Christians and demonstrate what real love looks like to those who do not know Jesus.

One of the special markings of this as a gift is an ability to give without burning out or experiencing the anxiety or stress from it that many people do. Of course, all Christians are called to be generous, just as we are all called to be hospitable, but some people truly live in it as a gift. As a result of living so generously, these people are quite often well-off financially. Do not mistake their generosity as a product of their abundance, but instead, see that their abundance is a product of their generosity.

In a related sense, I know my calling. I am not egotistical when I say I can pray for people and lives get changed financially. We are all called to fund the kingdom of God, so we pray things like, "God, if You want me to pay for that property, You supply, and we will do it!"

We have a big vision of what God wants done in this area. When you get extra money, remember, we have things to do for God. Be open and ready to receive the funding coming from open windows of heaven.

Everyone can employ this gift. Start small and allow God to work through you. Whenever you have a God-opportunity to give of your substance, ask Him what He wants you to do. Allow Him to direct you. Even though the church teaches the tithing concept, giving is not cut and dried with a specific formula. Allow God to direct you. Only God knows the blessings He has waiting for you if you are obedient.

This gift includes those working to help the needy, especially after disasters. Clothing and feeding the hungry or destitute may seem small, but to that hungry homeless person, you are an angel. Making a phone call to check on an elderly or homebound neighbor may be the highlight of their day. Even a smile or word of encouragement may be just the gift someone needs right now.

ENTREPRENEURSHIP

Certain people have a gift of entrepreneurship. While others try to build a business or organization, yet struggle, these people seem to be able to build anything. In fact, they may build several things and work to run them all at once!

They start one business, which fuels the startup money to begin another one. Each time they start a business, it gets off the ground, thrives, prospers, and continues to fuel more ventures in the future.

These people live the promise from God's Word that says, "Everything I touch shall prosper!" (see Deuteronomy 28:1–14). Testimonies of this gift over the last year have been phenomenal. Incomes have doubled through the covid crisis when other businesses and people were going bankrupt.

If you are someone whose income has suffered during this time, or if you have struggled to build a business, then you understand this truly is a gift of God, a grace and an anointing where He causes certain people to succeed in all they do. It has no more to do with the gifted person than any other spiritual gift.

You may read this and think, "Well, I certainly wish I had a gift of finances! I wish money came easy for me!" Let me strongly exhort you: Do not be jealous of this gift, but be zealous for it.

After all, God wants to bless you so you can become a greater blessing. Ask God for the gift, and even ask Him persistently, but ask Him to give you the wisdom of stewardship and generosity as well. Look to Him for good and see what He will do.

DREAMS, VISIONS, AND THEIR INTERPRETATION

Another gift is the ability to receive and interpret dreams and visions. Without a doubt, God sends dreams and visions to people. These are supernatural gifts from God that should cause men to seek Him for the interpretation. The Bible is full of dreams and visions that changed men's lives, gave direction, delivered people from death, gave understanding into great mysteries, and guided men and women throughout history (study the lives of Joseph, Daniel, and John, just for starters).

We should take our dreams seriously and expect God to speak to us through them. Don't be concerned if you don't have special dreams or visions. Instead, ask Him for the gifts He wants specifically for you.

If you are interested in interpretation of dreams and visions, check out Barbie Breathitt's many resources at www.barbiebreathitt.com. They are great!

DANCE

Throughout the Bible men and women used dancing as a means of worshipping God and releasing joy back to Him for all the great things He did for them. These dances are inspired by the Holy Spirit and glorify God, while encouraging men and women to live for God.

Often, dancers just appear in a service and contribute a wonderful element to the church worship. However, before you exit your seat to dance in the aisles of the church, make sure dancing is allowed. Some churches allow anointed dancing during any service. Others have strict rules about such activity. It may be allowed only during the Sunday night service or another designated meeting. Many churches don't allow dancing in any form. If you are attending a new church, take note of their accepted practices. Ask before you start. It should go without saying, however, that if you feel dancing is a gift God has given you, then you should probably find a church where it is encouraged.

This same form of worship includes flagging during a service. Dancing with flags can be glorious and a beautiful addition to worship. Again, some churches allow it, and some do not.

Seeing that churches take on such a wide array of practices when it comes to dancing or flagging, allow me to answer the basic question: is dancing and/or flagging scriptural? Oh, yes, they are both most definitely scriptural! Consider the following as just a few examples you could find in studying this out from Scripture:

Break forth with dancing! Make music and sing God's praises with the rhythm of drums! (Psalm 149:3 TPT)

You have given miraculous signs to those who love you. As we follow you, we fly the flag of truth, and all who love the truth will rally to it. Pause in his presence. (Psalm 60:4 TPT)

He has brought me to his banqueting place, and his banner over me is love [waving overhead to protect and comfort me]. (Song of Solomon 2:4 AMP)

Let them praise His name with dancing; let them sing praises to Him with the tambourine and lyre. (Psalm 149:3 AMP)

Praise him with drums and dancing! Praise him with loud clashing of cymbals! Praise him upon the high-sounding cymbals! (Psalm 150:4–5 TPT)

May there be shouts of joy when we hear the news of your victory, flags flying with praise to God for all that he has done for you. May he answer all your prayers! (Psalm 20:5 TLB)

Many Western believers come from conservatively stoic European cultures. We certainly don't reject our heritage if this is our background. We can, however, allow God to expand our expressions of worship beyond what our culture is perhaps comfortable with. Don't limit God.

GOD'S GENEROSITY IS ENDLESS

I could keep going on forever if I tried to list every single gift God could potentially give someone. His creativity, generosity, and desire to partner with us is that boundless. Instead, I will conclude by naming only a few more gifts I have seen active in people's lives.

One friend of mine can't do these other gifts I've already mentioned, but she is a computer whiz. It truly is a gift. A huge company had a glitch which no one could fix. She did it. Her ability is a gift from God.

Zack has a gift of videography. He can make gorgeous videos. He takes pictures and turns them into wonderful television programs. He has an eye for it to the point that it truly is a gift.

You may know Jonathan Williams. He is a gifted worship leader. A few years ago, he discovered he was also a gifted photographer. He can catch that perfect shot that tells a story. He found himself in the White House as a political photographer for several years. This ability did not come from training, but through gifting.

Julie Meyer is a gifted prophetic musician who has ministered at Joan Hunter Ministries many times over the last ten years. Her anointed ministry is prophetic music at the piano. This is different from being gifted at leading worship, because this working of the music ministry is spontaneous. It's often as though God's voice itself begins singing the melodies being released through the instruments. Miracles begin happening in that environment, and it is truly marvelous to see what God does in those times and places.

My oldest daughter, Charity, has a spiritual gift of writing. She is able to get books compiled, edited, and published in a truly rare and special way. She uses her gift as the head of Lifewise Publications.

What is your gift? Is it cooking, sewing, or designing? Is it speaking or organization? Maybe it's coordinating or administration. All of these are special gifts from God.

Whatever your gift is, steward it as a gift from God. Ask Him what purpose He has for that gift in your life, then get things in alignment with that purpose. You will almost always find that, as you faithfully serve God with your gift, God will increase your gift, expand the area of influence you have with your gift, or simply give you more gifts.

thoughts to ponder:

* What additional gifts from God are active in your life?

* Think about people in your life who have impacted your walk with the Lord. What gifts do you see being used within their ministry?

* How can you activate God's gifts in your family, your church, and with your friends?

* What gifts to you specifically want to develop?

* How can you use your gifts to draw others to faith in Jesus Christ?

chapter 7

MORE WAYS TO PARTNER WITH GOD

Many other subjects often come up when anyone talks about gifts of the Spirit. These can be just as important to understand as the gifts themselves because they help us understand how to partner with the Holy Spirit more effectively.

A part of this is simply because God working in our world often looks or seems strange. That doesn't mean it's strange to Him. He lives in heaven where everything is supernatural compared to what we know on earth. If we had just one peek into what continually surrounds God every day, then we might not think what He does on earth is so unusual. The truth is, it's just unusual for us, at least when we first encounter it.

Just because something is strange, however, doesn't mean it's from God. I want to introduce you to some of the spiritual dynamics and ways the Holy Spirit manifests so they don't take you by surprise. I also want to give you biblical basis for it all so you aren't shaken, but remain free to continue partnering with the Holy Spirit to win souls and minister His love, goodness, and mercy.

ANOINTING

A subject that is very similar to spiritual gifting is the subject of anointing. If you understand that speaking in tongues is allowing God to speak through you for a specific situation or time, I want to explain His anointing in the same way. Just as you allow God to use your voice to speak, pray, or teach, you can allow Him to use your music, writing, painting, or dancing in the same way.

You may have learned some of the basics of playing the piano, for example. With His anointing, you may find yourself playing music you have never studied. It seems to just flow through your hands onto the keyboard. The same principle can apply to any instrument or activity you participate in. You may have a certain competency in an area, but with God's anointing, your talent or gift increases to a more excellent level.

Ask for God's anointing on whatever you do. Allow His Holy Spirit to bless you with His abilities working through you. The Holy Spirit will bless any and every gift you have been blessed with. There may be many, many more gifts just waiting for you to open and accept. Just seek God for His anointing and the gifts He desires for you.

Not everyone is an apostle or a prophet or a teacher.
Not everyone performs miracles or has gifts of healing

or speaks in tongues or interprets tongues. But you should all constantly boil over with passion in seeking the higher gifts. And now I will show you a superior way to live that is beyond comparison! (1 Corinthians 12:29–31 TPT)

You are the body of the Anointed One, and each of you is a unique and vital part of it. (1 Corinthians 12:27 TPT)

THE BAPTISM OF FIRE

You may have heard about the baptism of fire, but what is it? Is it scriptural?

I am happy to tell you, yes, it is scriptural. In fact, John the Baptist promised that Jesus would give it to us just as He would give us the baptism of the Holy Spirit:

"I baptize you with water for repentance. But after me comes one who is more powerful than I, whose sandals I am not worthy to carry. He will baptize you with the Holy Spirit and fire." (Matthew 3:11 NIV)

What happens in the baptism of fire? Occasionally, I experience this as something special that happens during a service. For instance, someone will get an extra boost from the Holy Spirit. I mean that they may get an extraordinary revelation about their calling from God. They suddenly know that they know they are to become a pastor or missionary. Maybe a special prayer will instantly get answered. Don't feel slighted if you don't experience this phenomenon, as it doesn't happen to everyone.

On the day Pentecost was being fulfilled, all the disciples were gathered in one place. Suddenly they heard the sound of a violent blast of wind rushing into the house from out of the heavenly realm. The roar of the wind was so overpowering it was all anyone could bear! Then all at once a pillar of fire appeared before their eyes. It separated into tongues of fire that engulfed each one of them. They were all filled and equipped with the Holy Spirit and were inspired to speak in tongues—empowered by the Spirit to speak in languages they had never learned! (Acts 2:1–4 TPT)

SLAIN IN THE SPIRIT

You may have heard comments such as, "I've been under the power," or, "They fell backwards when the minister prayed for them." These comments are trying to explain a very real phenomenon we see in both the Bible and present-day experience but is still difficult to explain.

We often call this phenomenon being "slain in the Spirit." The Bible does not use the words "slain in the Spirit," but it does mention people who fell into a deep sleep or trance. These words can also be used to refer to being "under the power."

My mom and dad first became aware of this phenomenon of being slain in the Spirit, or falling under the power, in the ministry of the late Kathryn Kuhlman. Their introduction to people being slain in the Spirit was watching twenty-four Catholic nuns all fall down at one of Miss Kuhlman's services. They knew it was of God!

Mom explained to me later that, at the time, she wondered

how Miss Kuhlman did that. The next thing Mom knew, Miss Kuhlman was pointing directly at her. Mom stepped out and floated to the floor like a feather.

Mom felt nothing specific. God did not speak to her; but she knew she had been with Jesus. In that split second of time when Mom was under the power, God broke down every barrier she had about the baptism of the Holy Spirit. A short time after that, Dad and Mom both accepted the baptism of the Holy Spirit and began to pray in tongues.

AWESOME AND SUPERNATURAL

For whatever reason, many people find this experience so strange that they just can't imagine it being something God does. What we find in Scripture, however, is that God has been doing this very thing since nearly the beginning of time.

The book of Genesis records the first time anyone went under the power, saying that Adam fell into a deep sleep. God gave Adam a spiritual anesthetic, so to speak. While Adam was under the power, God removed a rib from him and formed a woman. People who are under the power look just like they are sleeping. God often ministers something special during these times, such as a healing or a special anointing.

Moving on in Scripture, Genesis 15 describes Abraham having a similar experience to the one Adam had, as a deep sleep fell on him, followed by a profound history-changing vision in which God covenanted with Abraham for future generations.

Later, 2 Chronicles 5:13–14 tells us of people who were unable to stand in the presence of God. Two chapters later, in

7:2, other people were unable to enter the temple because of God's glory.

Continuing on, Daniel 10:9–10 (NKJV) says:

> "Yet I heard the sound of his words; and while I heard the sound of his words I was in a deep sleep on my face, with my face to the ground. Suddenly, a hand touched me, which made me tremble on my knees and on the palms of my hands."

God not only took Daniel under the power, but put him back on his feet! Ezekiel records a similar encounter twice in the first three chapters of his book where the Spirit of God needed to lift Him back up after he fell down in God's presence. Clearly, there are simply times in God's presence when it is impossible to remain standing!

GOD IS THE SAME

If we see God working in this way in the Old Testament and in our modern day, it should not surprise us to find it in the New Testament as well. One of the most powerful examples comes from the moment of Jesus' arrest in the garden:

> Jesus, knowing full well what was about to happen, went out to the garden entrance to meet them. Stepping forward, he asked, "Who are you looking for?"
>
> "Jesus of Nazareth," they replied. (Now Judas, the traitor, was among them.)

He replied, "I am he." And the moment Jesus spoke the words, "I am he," the mob fell backward to the ground! (John 18:4–6 TPT)

The Pharisees had sent a squad of soldiers to arrest Jesus and every one of them fell backward under the power of God.

Other soldiers, this time a trained cohort of Romans, fell under God's power just three days later outside Jesus' tomb:

After the Sabbath ended, at the first light of dawn on the first day of the week, Mary Magdalene and the other Mary went to take a look at the tomb. Suddenly, the earth shook violently beneath their feet as the angel of the Yahweh descended from heaven. Lightning flashed around him and his robe was dazzling white! The guards were stunned and terrified—lying motionless like dead men. Then the angel walked up to the tomb, rolled away the stone, and sat on top of it! (Matthew 28:1–4 TPT)

The examples just keep going. Just watch the history God shaped through these next few examples, starting with a few years later when the apostle Peter fell into a trance while he was praying:

Peter went up on the flat roof of his house to pray. It was noon and he was hungry, but while lunch was being prepared, he fell into a trance. (Acts 10:9–10 TPT)

Many believers are afraid of the word trance because they associate it solely with demonic religions and their practices, but here we see that God had a very special message to give Peter and He chose to deliver it to him by using a trance. Also, Peter was not up on the roof to talk to the devil; he was up there to pray, to talk to God. We should know that if a believer is fully seeking God, God won't let them find Satan instead (see Luke 11:13).

Similar experiences twice changed Paul's life—once by saving his life, and the other by saving his soul:

"After I returned to Jerusalem, I was praying in the Temple and fell into a trance." (Acts 22:17 NLT)

God spoke to Paul in this trance to warn him about the danger of staying in Jerusalem, commanding him to go abroad instead, even to the Gentiles. This wasn't the first time Paul had been struck to the ground under God's power, however. The first time it happened to him set his life on a completely new path:

As he was nearing Damascus on this mission, suddenly a brilliant light from heaven spotted down upon him! He fell to the ground and heard a voice saying to him, "Saul! Saul! Why are you persecuting me?" "Who is speaking, sir?" Paul asked. And the voice replied, "I am Jesus, the one you are persecuting! Now get up and go into the city and await my further instructions." The men with Paul stood speechless with surprise, for they heard the sound of someone's voice but saw no one! As Paul picked himself up off the ground, he found that he was blind. (Acts 9:3–9 TLB)

Saul had murdered many Christians, yet he was suddenly unable to stand in the presence of Almighty God. He didn't recover until he had walked several days in total obedience to God's voice.

Finally, we see a third apostle fall under God's power at the beginning of the book of Revelation:

I was on the island of Patmos, exiled there for preaching the Word of God and for telling what I knew about Jesus Christ. It was the Lord's Day and I was worshiping, when suddenly I heard a loud voice behind me, a voice that sounded like a trumpet blast… When I saw him, I fell at his feet as dead. (Rev. 1:9–10, 17 TLB)

If the truth of a matter is established by two or three witnesses, what does it say when Scripture tells us of at least eleven people or groups of people, some of whom fell under God's power more than once? Surely it tells us that we should not be surprised to see God still work in this way today.

EXAMPLES FROM MODERN DAY

In fact, we find God does often work this way today when people are in close contact with Him. This includes Jesus and His Holy Spirit.

In one of Mom and Dad's meetings in Toronto, Canada, Treena Kerr toppled off her chair and lay prostrate on the floor. They didn't even touch her husband, Graham, and he fell under the power of God as well. Later, in that same meeting, seven rows of people went under the power of God all at once.

A friend of mine tells of an experience she had, saying:

We were in Duluth, Minnesota, to see Charles and Frances Hunter. They were speaking at a school auditorium. It was packed. Everyone was standing after a session of praise and worship. Frances was at the pulpit when she raised her hand and waved it over the audience. Suddenly, everyone in the audience was falling backwards into their seats. Many came forward later to tell of the miracles that happened while they were under the power of God. The room was alive with Him! When my husband stood up, he realized his chronic back pain was completely gone!

Why would God choose to work through such an unusual method? What is His purpose in it?

Well, many people are healed physically or emotionally, baptized in the Holy Spirit, or have visions. Some people hear God speaking to them about things specific to them. Some receive a baptism of fire and are forever changed. Many people are delivered of evil spirits. Thousands of people have been delivered of cigarettes, alcohol, or drugs when slain in the Spirit.

In other words, God uses this method for just about any-thing He may want to do, especially when He wants to move very directly in us with less (or sometimes no) resistance from us. Mom and Dad often reported, "The greatest thing that we notice is the desire it gives a person for reading the Word of God!"

While we may not understand everything about being slain in the Spirit, it is important for us to remember to respect and stand in awe of the presence of God. The power of God is not a plaything!

I have been asked, "How do you do this?" I always answer that I have nothing to do with it. I just pray for people and fol-low God's leading, but I don't know why anybody falls down. It is God's power, not mine.

Many others ask, "Why do some fall and some don't?"

There could be many reasons for this. Honestly, some people resist God working in them through this way and God chooses not to violate their will. Others seem to have an anoint-ing from God to stand in His presence even when everyone else falls down. It isn't that God's power doesn't touch them; it's just that it works differently in them.

The bottom line to all this is that God is sovereign. We do know He works through this phenomenon, but we don't understand all the mysteries of it. We can ask Him directly someday, and in the meantime remember that He knows what we need and when we need it.

It is the same Holy Spirit who continues to distribute many different varieties of gifts. The Lord Yahweh is one, and he is the one who apportions to believers different varieties of ministries. The same God distributes different kinds of miracles that accomplish different results through each believer's gift and ministry as he energizes and activates them. Each believer is given continuous revelation by the Holy Spirit to benefit not just himself but all. (1 Corinthians 12: 4–7 TPT)

thoughts to ponder:

* What is the anointing?

* What have you asked God to anoint?

* Have you ever been slain in the Spirit?

* How does it help you to see examples of people being slain in the Spirit in both the Old and New Testaments?

* Which story of being slain in the Spirit stands out to you most? What stands out to you about it?

* How would you explain why God makes people fall down sometimes?

chapter 8

DEVELOP
YOUR GIFTS

*Y*ou may have heard the expression "walk on water" as a reference to trying something that's considered impossible. I want to take that expression a step further. I encourage you to "walk on spiritual water."

Believe God's promises. Believe Jesus' promises. Take what you have learned to this point and start to exercise the various gifts. When you step out with faith, God will expand not only your understanding, but also the results.

Gifts are a partnership between God and man. Cooperation is essential. Like many things, learning how and when to use a gift allows it to become stronger and more effective when you minister.

Scripture clearly and strongly exhorts us to use our gifts:

God's marvelous grace imparts to each one of us varying gifts. So if God has given you the grace-gift of prophecy, activate your gift by using the proportion of faith you have to prophesy. If your grace-gift is serving, then thrive in serving others well. If you have the grace-gift of teaching, then be actively teaching and training others. If you have the grace-gift of encouragement, then use it often to encourage others. If you have the grace-gift of giving to meet the needs of others, then may you prosper in your generosity without any fanfare. If you have the gift of leadership, be passionate about your leadership. And if you have the gift of showing compassion, then flourish in your cheerful display of compassion. (Romans 12:6–8 TPT)

Ignoring or neglecting your gifts will cause them to fade. It is like getting a valuable birthday gift and placing it on the top shelf of your closet to gather dust. It is there and available, but you aren't getting any benefit from it. You don't enjoy it. You don't use it. It could be a million dollars or the key to a valuable new car, but it lays dormant and powerless.

Whether you just prayed for your spiritual regeneration through the Holy Spirit or whether you received Him many years ago, it is time to open the box, release His Spirit, and allow His valuable power to flow through you.

ACTIVATE YOUR GIFT

The exhortation I am giving you now is nothing new. Paul said the same thing to his spiritual son, Timothy:

Don't minimize the powerful gift that operates in your life, for it was imparted to you by the laying on of hands of the elders and was activated through the prophecy they spoke over you. (1 Timothy 4:14 TPT)

My suggestion to help you in this is to open the Bible to God's promises. They were written to and for you. Stand in front of a mirror and start reading those promises out loud while looking at yourself. In essence, you are prophesying to yourself. You don't have to wait to find an anointed prophet to speak over you. Start by exercising God's promises from His anointed Word and minister to yourself.

Ministering to yourself in this way is a great start. Then, at some point, you must take the next step by ministering to others and praying for them. A bottled-up stream ceases to be life-giving, so do not bottle up the flow of the Holy Spirit in and through you. Instead, release it to others, as Scripture tells us:

As each one has received a gift, minister it to one another, as good stewards of the manifold grace of God. (1 Peter 4:10 NKJV)

In all you do, in ministering to both yourself and others, continually pursue intimacy with Jesus through the Holy Spirit.

My heart is always full and overflowing with thanks to God for you as I constantly remember you in my prayers. I pray that the Father of glory, the God of our Lord Jesus Christ, would impart to you the riches of the Spirit of wisdom and the Spirit of revelation to know him through your deepening intimacy with him. (Ephesians 1:16–17 TPT)

The closer you stay to God, the more He can use you. You will recognize His voice and be prepared to minister as He directs. You may even get addicted to being used by the Father, Son, and Holy Ghost in your everyday activities. Your Christian walk will never be more exciting.

I don't say this will always be easy or convenient. It will not always be either easy or convenient. It has been especially challenging in the recent past as I am writing this but walk in obedience to the Lord anyway. Stay in His Word. Listen for His voice; He is always speaking to you. As you obey Him, you will see your gifts grow, your intimacy with God deepen, and the fruit of your life multiply. Allow Him to continue showering your life with more blessings.

Now you have every grace and blessing; every spiritual gift and power for doing his will are yours during this time of waiting for the return of our Lord Jesus Christ. (1 Corinthians 1:7 TLB)

LEARN FROM ONE ANOTHER

Practicing anything new is, by definition, new territory, and any time we enter new territory it is helpful to have someone with us to confirm we are going the right way. It is no different with spiritual gifts. Simply put, we will go farther and become stronger when we practice our gifts in a community with others and are able to learn and receive from each other.

I yearn to come and be face-to-face with you and get to know you. For I long to impart to you some spiritual gift that will empower you to stand strong in your faith. (Romans 1:11 TPT)

What's more, your testimony soars to a new level with the baptism of the Holy Spirit and the activation of His gifts. Each word you share with another now has His power and anointing. Every conversation will have new meaning. Learning from others will seem to be so easy with the revelation from the Spirit in action.

Connect with a minister, pastor, mentor, or leader who already operates in the gifts of the Spirit. Listen carefully and watch their actions. Then, in turn, they can watch you and guide you through your learning process.

Even the simplest lessons are learned faster when you have an example to follow. For instance, believe me when I say that long and flowery prayers are not necessary. I have had many people get healed, for example, with the simplest of words, such as, "Be healed, in Jesus' name!" Even Jesus often ministered with a few words. You can learn this from me just by reading this, but most believers start out thinking God will only hear them if they pray lots of words. This is just one very basic example of the benefit of finding a teacher or mentor to help you grow.

There are many good teachers on television, radio, and online. Many of my meetings are available for you to enjoy, learn, and share 24/7. Conferences are great as well as more intimate gatherings. Remember also the many excellent books that are available, but ultimately, go where God guides you.

There is always more to learn. Learning never stops. God is revealing new things to His children all the time. Be open to receive from others. Just test what you hear and line it up with God's Word.

AUTHENTICITY

This testing of all you hear is very important. Even the Scriptures caution believers to use discernment when being taught or mentored by others. I am sure you have heard the term "wolf in sheep's clothing." Be aware and determine for yourself if the words being said to you match up with the Bible. Does the message ring true with your spirit, or do you question the validity of the speaker?

> But now you are meeting people who claim to speak messages from the Spirit of God. How can you know whether they are really inspired by God or whether they are fakes? Here is the test: no one speaking by the power of the Spirit of God can curse Jesus, and no one can say, "Jesus is Lord," and really mean it, unless the Holy Spirit is helping him. (1 Corinthians 12:3 TLB)

> It's crucial that we keep a firm grip on what we've heard so that we don't drift off. If the old message delivered by the angels was valid and nobody got away with anything, do you think we can risk neglecting this latest message, this magnificent salvation? First of all, it was delivered in person by the Master, then accurately passed on to us by those who heard it from him. All

the while God was validating it with gifts through the Holy Spirit, all sorts of signs and miracles, as he saw fit. (Hebrews 2:1–4 MSG)

Listen, learn, and test the spirit of the speaker no matter who they are. Direct any questions you have to your mentor. Don't repeat or speak anything contrary to what God wants you to speak. Remember, He wants you to walk in truth, love, and mercy.

As a simple example, I have heard people prophesy doom and gloom and evil over a group of Christians, but prophecy is to encourage and exhort, not condemn. Be careful what you say to another. Speak in love like Jesus did.

LAY HANDS ON ONE ANOTHER

Just as David learned to encourage himself in the Lord, we have to stir up the many gifts God has given us. Remember, we do not all receive the same gifts. This means you can share what God has blessed you with by laying hands on another in need. There is also strength in agreement. That fact alone should encourage you to lay hands on one another.

Therefore I remind you to stir up the gift of God which is in you through the laying on of my hands. (2 Timothy 1:6 NKJV)

Laying hands on another person is not limited to a service even though that is where you will witness it being done most often. Hugging someone or shaking hands with another person also allows God's power to pass through you to them. Maybe you have a family member who needs a touch but is unwilling to even recognize that God heals through a person. You can certainly be thinking in tongues while you hug them or kiss them in your usual manner of greeting. These days even an elbow bump can be used when someone is unwilling to have any greater degree of physical contact.

All the gifts are activated by faith, no matter how you receive them. Faith is believing not just with your mind, but with your heart and spirit in agreement with God and His promises. His promises are activated as you exercise this belief. Hope becomes substance. Be sensitive to what God tells you to do, then *do it*. You have all the faith you need if you have faith to hear God. Faith cannot be attained by man's efforts—it is a gift.

So then faith cometh by hearing, and hearing by the word of God. (Romans 10:17 KJV)

Looking unto Jesus the author and finisher of our faith; who for the joy that was set before him endured the cross, despising the shame, and is set down at the right hand of the throne of God. (Hebrews 12:2 KJV)

Faith can be developed as it is exercised for daily and special miracles as we show that we really do trust God for humanly impossible acts. As I said before when I wrote on the gift of faith, Hebrews 11 is a great chapter to read if you want to learn more about faith.

As you grow in your gifts among a community of believers,

or even along with your mentor, it is important to encourage one another. This will happen naturally to some extent, but even more as you become intentional about it.

> For I long to visit you so that I can impart to you the faith that will help your church grow strong in the Lord. Then, too, I need your help, for I want not only to share my faith with you but to be encouraged by yours: Each of us will be a blessing to the other. (Romans 1:11–12 TLB)

Every testimony you share will encourage others to step out in faith to use their gifts. Even your mentor/leader/pastor will be encouraged by hearing about your success.

We also at Joan Hunter Ministries would love to hear your testimonies. You can share these with us through the contact page on our website, www.joanhunter.org/contact, or by emailing us at info@joanhunter.org. Please let us know what happens as you step out on your new journey filled with Holy Spirit gifts and God's power. Your testimony is a big thank you to the JHM staff and volunteers who work so hard to minister to you.

BE TOTALLY ABSORBED BY GOD

Your goal is to walk with, talk with, and listen to God through His Holy Spirit. To be more like Jesus, you should be willingly and completely in the Spirit at all times. Submit to the will of God. Remember, all His gifts are activated and operated by faith.

If you are obedient to God's will, evidence follows. Signs, wonders, and miracles will become a normal part of your life. What's even more, you will be filled with the fruit of the Spirit:

> But the fruit produced by the Holy Spirit within you is divine love in all its varied expressions: joy that overflows, peace that subdues, patience that endures, kindness in action, a life full of virtue, faith that prevails, gentleness of heart, and strength of spirit. Never set the law above these qualities, for they are meant to be limitless. (Galatians 5:22 TPT)

Ready or not, jump in and begin doing what you can. Pray and ask the Holy Spirit what gifts He has given you. Ask Him for any specific assignments He has for you and your gifts. Look for ways you can serve Him with your gifts even when you don't feel led specifically.

Do those things, and this is the life that waits for you on the other side of obediently walking in the Spirit. It is a life that looks like Jesus, a life of explosive power, fully able to release God's love, mercy, and salvation wherever you go.

thoughts to ponder:

* What questions about the gift of the Spirit have been answered in this book? What others do you still have?

* How do you plan to develop your gifts?

* Who do you think will benefit from the information you have learned?

* Who do you know that exemplifies best the fruit of the Spirit operating in their lives?

.

* What fruit do you desire to operate in your life?

FOR MORE INFORMATION ABOUT THE GIFTS

If you still have questions about the gifts of the Spirit, please contact the Joan Hunter Ministries office. See www.joanhunter.org/contact for our contact information. We would love to pray with you and offer further information. We are all learning more every day as God's revelations are revealed and released.

Please document your journey for yourself and for your family as a testimony for the future, and maybe for your own book.

ABOUT THE AUTHOR

Joan Hunter's genuine approach and candid delivery enables her to connect intimately with people from all walks of life. Her focus is to train and equip believers to take the healing power of God beyond the 4 walls of the church and into the 4 corners of the earth!

Joan ministers the Gospel with manifestations of supernatural signs and wonders in healing school sessions, miracle services, conferences, and churches around the world. Being sensitive to the Holy Spirit, Joan speaks prophetically in the services, releasing personal and corporate prophetic ministry to those in attendance.

At the young age of twelve, Joan dedicated her heart to the Lord and has faithfully served him from that day to this. She has uncompromising faith and dedication to the call of God on her life. She exhibits a sincere desire to see the body of Christ set free in their body, mind, soul, spirit, and finances.

Joan is a compassionate minister, dynamic teacher, an accomplished author, and an anointed healing evangelist.

Joan has ministered in countries all over the world and has been on numerous television and radio appearances. She has been featured on Sid Roth's *It's Supernatural, My New Day, The Jim Bakker Show, Faith with Katie Souza,* and on *Today with Marilyn* (Hickey) *and Sarah.* Joan hosts a powerful and exciting show of her own called *Miracles Happen!*

She has authored more than twenty-five books and has recorded teachings that will encourage you and teach you how to pray for the sick and see them recover. Books and teachings are available to order through joanhunter.org or joanhunter.ca. Some resources are available as digital downloads through Amazon.com and iTunes. You can watch Joan at www.Miracles Happen.tv and on the Joan Hunter Ministries' YouTube page.

Joan Hunter and her husband, Kelley, live northwest of Houston, Texas. Together, they have 4 daughters, 4 sons, 3 son's-in-laws and 7 grandchildren. Joan is the daughter of the Happy Hunters, Charles and Frances Hunter.

INDEX

INDEX

notes

notes

notes

notes

notes

notes

notes